The
Oxidation
of Grief

The Oxidation of Grief

Reflections on Adult Sibling Loss

Maria Piantanida

Learning Moments Press
Pittsburgh, PA

The Oxidation of Grief: Reflections on Adult Sibling Loss
Published by Learning Moments Press
Pittsburgh, PA 15235
learningmomentspress.com

ISBN-13: 9780997648843

BISAC Subject:
FAM14000 Family & Relationships/Death, Grief, Bereavement

Onix Audience Code:
01 General/Trade

Book Layout:
Mike Murray, pearhouse.com

For my sister Lilly
who lived with zest and
died with grace, dignity and courage.

Contents

PROLOGUE

Gone Before Their Time

It happened to Ted Kennedy and Caroline Kennedy Schlossberg. It happened to Venus and Serena Williams and Dan Jansen. It happened to Queen Latifah, Barry Gibb of the Bee Gees, Bruce Willis, and Kellie Martin. It happened to Katie Couric.[1] And it happened to me.

Rationally, I know fame, money, and power offer no immunity from pain, suffering and death. Yet, I am always shocked to read that the brother or sister of a celebrity has died in the prime of life. While I would wish such tragedy on no one, I take some comfort in knowing that I am not alone in my loss.

Around the time I turned 40, I began to scan the death notices in my local paper. Mainly I was checking for the names of anyone in the small town where I had grown up. With increasing frequency, I would spot the name of an elementary school teacher, an acquaintance of my parents, or someone who had been a customer in my father's pharmacy. These were elderly individuals who had reached or surpassed the threshold of normal life expectancy—living

---

1 Ted Kennedy survived the loss of brothers John and Robert. John F. Kennedy, Jr., the brother of Carolyn Kennedy Schlossberg died at age 38 when the private plane he was piloting crashed. Yetunde Price, the oldest sister of tennis champions Venus and Serena Williams was shot to death at the age of 31. Speed skater and Olympic Gold medalist, Dan Jensen, lost his older sister, Jane, from leukemia. Rapper and actress Queen Latifah lost her older brother Lancelot—he died in the crash of a motor cycle that had been a gift from his sister. Barry Gibb has lost three brothers—Robin, Maurice and Andy. Actor Bruce Willis lost his younger brother to pancreatic cancer at age 42. Actress Kellie Martin lost her sister, Heather, age 19, from lupus erythematosus. Katie Couric's sister Emily died from pancreatic cancer at the age of 54.

well into their 70s, 80s, or even 90s. Occasionally, however, my attention would be drawn to the name of a total stranger. Invariably, it was their age of death—39, 46, 52, 61—that caused me to take note of their passing. Still, I thought of these as isolated instances, anomalies in the expectable progression from cradle to grave. This changed in the instant that my younger sister, Lilly was diagnosed with kidney cancer at the age of 49.

In the late fall of 1998 and winter of 1999, Lilly underwent two surgeries. The first was to remove her ovaries and a growth that turned out to be benign. The second was to remove her left kidney and the tumors that turned out to be cancerous. "It was a stage 2 cancer," Lilly told me. "The main tumor was encapsulated. The surrounding lymph nodes were clear. But it had gone into the renal vein."

"She's dead," I thought, but asked, "So what is the next step? Chemo?"

"No. They say I need to come back in a year for a screening, but there isn't any chemo."

My sister's tone was very positive and implied there was nothing to worry about. The implication seemed to be that they had caught it in time so no further treatment was indicated. This didn't fit with "It had invaded the renal vein."

There are three physicians in my family. Normally when a health related question arises, I call one or more of them for clarification. This time I made no phone calls. I couldn't ask a question that I couldn't bear to hear answered.

On Easter Sunday, I called my older sister, Linda, and her family to say hello. At one point, my brother-in-law, Bob, a doctor, said, "It's not good about Lilly."

I remembered then why I hadn't called for several weeks. Steeling myself, I asked, "What about Lilly?"

"She'll enjoy about 18 months of good health. Then the cancer will metastasize to her lungs. They may be able to cut it out. Maybe not. Then she'll die."

In response to my follow up questions, I learned that the second tumor growing in the renal vein had been 5 centimeters. This was a Stage 4b out of 5 cancer scenario. Tumors shed cells, my brother-in-law explained, and in this case the cells would have been shed directly into the blood stream. No chemo is effective against kidney cancer. That's why no follow-up treatment was indicated. Statistically speaking, the five year survival rates for kidney cancer are grim.

The thought of losing my baby sister was unbearable. Fear for her and the suffering that lay ahead; sorrow for all of life's pleasures that she would be losing; sorrow for my losing her—the prospect of such pain and grief was unendurable. Yet, others have endured the loss of a sibling. Even a quick inventory of my closest friends brought to mind two whose brothers had literally dropped dead of heart attacks and one whose sister had succumbed to cancer. If they could survive the unendurable, I supposed I could, too. I began to wonder how others did cope with the loss of a sibling in the prime of life.

In the winter and spring of 1999, when we were still hoping against hope that Lilly might find a miracle cure, I began to interview men and women who had survived the death of a brother or sister. One woman, a minister, had lost her brother over 30 years earlier. This was a much longer span of grief than that experienced by the others with whom I had spoken. I was curious whether the quality of grief changed over time. Upon hearing my question, Rachel responded, "Oh, yeah. I think oxidation takes care of some of it."

The image of oxidizing copper came immediately to mind. The patina with its subtle shadings of light and dark green, its flecks of white and gray, its threads of reddish brown. This, it seemed to me, was an apt metaphor for grief. Original streaks of raw anguish still bleed through to the surface. But there are softer, more mellow spots as well. Grief, muted by the passage of time, gentled by memory. Layers of sadness, bittersweet remembrances, and regrets intermingling with past and present joy.

Part 1 of this book comprises a collection of essays written over a span of 16 years. The essays trace the oxidation of my own grief. I wrote the essay, *Small Comforts* in the months following my sister's death, a time before oxidation began. Or perhaps, oxidation was occurring as my thoughts and feelings flowed onto paper. I felt more at peace once the essay was done. Yet, the existential themes that weave throughout *Small Comforts* were not so easily put to rest. Over the years, subsequent writings reflect my on-going struggles with questions of belief and doubt, good and evil, grief and guilt, anxiety and joy, and the meaning of life and death. Thus, *Small Comforts* serves not only as the earliest and rawest expression of grief, but also as an introduction to themes that replay in subsequent essays.

In the two years following Lilly's death, I lapsed into an odd state of irritability and lethargy. On the surface, I seemed placid enough, but the slightest misspoken word (usually from my husband) evoked angry retorts and tears. Finding little to elicit either my intellectual or emotional engagement I spent hours watching mindless television and reading happy-ending books. Still, in the background, was a nagging sense of obligation to "do something" with the interviews I had gathered. Finally, in January 2005, a lifelong learning program at the University of Pittsburgh gave me the opportunity to audit an undergraduate class on death and dying. This, I hoped, would provide me with a theoretical framework for interpreting the personal experiences of my interviewees. Early in the course, a clinical psychologist- researcher gave a lecture on the stages of death and dying, including his own efforts to determine what precisely might move people through these stages in a more predictable and expeditious way. THIS evoked both the irritation and engagement that so often precipitate my need to write. *Circling in An Eddy of Grief* is my attempt to challenge the privileged position of scientific research, even in realms where wisdom, not certitude, is called for.

In the fall of 1999 when Lilly's cancer diagnosis was confirmed, my mother turned 90 and began her final nine-year descent through dementia. By the time I wrote the *Eddy* essay, grief for her mingled with grief for Lilly and with reactivated memories of my father's death. These feelings and memories eventually coalesced into two vignettes—*On the Death of a Sister* and *Coming Face to Face with Death*. Writing the former helped to bridge the emotional distance

I had long maintained between my mother and me. The latter eased the grip of guilt and shame I had experienced when my father died as well as the haunting images of his face and Lilly's in death.

In my early adult years, I had no patience for gardening. The time-lag between planting seeds and enjoying results was too long; I wanted instant gratification. And weeding was so boring. After Lilly's death and during my mother's decline, however, gardening gave me the appearance of doing something useful while allowing my mind to wander aimlessly. Accounts of random deaths often insinuated themselves into my more innocuous musings. The capriciousness of catastrophe never fails to shock me and fuels a lifelong anxiety about blink-of-an-eye disasters. The confluence of these thoughts with my gardening activities led to the writing of *I Kill Earthworms* and *On The Edge*.

The impetus for the final two essays was an invitation from Peter Willis, a friend and colleague, to write a piece for a project he had in mind. He had read a book called *Illness: The Cry of the Flesh* by Havi Carel which had touched him deeply enough to propose that others also read the book and write a response to it. I'm not sure what happened after I sent Peter some preliminary reactions. I dimly recall that he was (unpleasantly?) surprised that I had found the book somewhat irritating. In any event, I did not hear more from Peter about his progress with the project and assumed that either my piece was no longer wanted or he had abandoned the idea. So my notes languished until a now forgotten impulse brought me back to them. In *Shopping for Steak at Home Depot*, I explore my longing for medical professionals to respond with empathy to the angst engendered by life-threatening illness. In *Where Do We Turn for Comfort?*, I struggle with my own inadequacies in talking with loved ones about death.

In Part 2 of the book, I present stories of sibling loss crafted from my interviews with friends and strangers. Interestingly, several individuals mentioned their annoyance with books that seemed to prescribe specific time-frames and ways of coping with their grief. As one woman put it, "I want to do it in my own way, in my own time.

If I still want to be crying when I'm 50, so what? I miss my brother and it's my way of remembering him." In hearing such comments and in my own reading of literature on death and dying, I eventually realized I had encountered no books that dealt specifically with grief for the death of an adult sibling. Because I had found comfort in hearing the stories of siblings who had endured what I feared would be unendurable, I am sharing their stories in the hope that they may bring comfort to others.

PART 1

1

Small Comforts

LESSONS FROM
MY SISTER'S BEDSIDE

My sister, Lilly, died the night of March 26, 2003, sometime between 9:00 and midnight, while her husband Tom and I were asleep. She left in the darkness punctuated only by the gentle snores of their yellow Labrador, Giles, and the rhythmic hiss of her oxygen concentrator.

I fear I failed her in those final moments. Throughout the long months of her dying, I had imagined sitting at her side, holding her hand, stroking her hair as her breathing trailed into infinite stillness. But I went to bed that night, thinking that her dwindling life was still measured in half days, not half hours. At 9:00 p.m., as we had administered medicine to calm her racing heart and ease her gasping lungs, Tom and I had looked for the telltale signs of imminent death as described by the hospice nurse earlier in the day. Blue mottling on her feet and legs; skin cooling to the touch—these were not present. Or did I not want to see them? The end was coming, but not now, not this night, not before the stroke of midnight.

At two in the morning, after the medical examiner had finished his paperwork, after the hospice nurse had inventoried and destroyed the unused medications, after the transport company had come and gone, Tom began to dismantle the hospital bed where Lilly had lain for over four months. Such a practical task. Or was it symbolic—acknowledging that the war, like all of the battles against the implacable cancer, had been lost. Perhaps it was simply too painful to sleep next to the vacant bed. I didn't know and couldn't ask. So I just joined in the task. I began to strip the bed and was shocked that my sister's warmth still lingered in the pillows, sheets and blankets. A story she had written as a child flashed up out of memory—a child lying in a coffin, calling out in confused desperation to her parents—"Mom, Dad what's happening? Can't you see I'm still here? Why isn't anyone talking to me? Where are you going? Why are you leaving me behind?" I pushed the memory down as I always do, repelled by the horror it evokes. I could not talk with her about the story when she wrote it decades ago. I had not been able to ask about her fears as death loomed closer and closer.

So I fear I failed her in the end, letting her go without a final good-bye. Yet, I wonder if that was the only way she could leave. Starting in September of 2002, I began alternating my time between Reno where my sister lived and Pittsburgh where obligations of work and family required my presence. Each time I left for home, I dissolved in private tears, inconsolable at the prospect of saying good-bye. By the end of January, the hospice nurse projected that Lilly might have only 7 – 10 days left. So when I returned to Reno that time, I planned to stay till the end. As a week or two turned into four, then five, then six, seven, eight weeks, some people expressed concern for me. Didn't I want to take a break, come home for a while, take care of some of my own needs? The truth of the matter was, I couldn't say good-bye to my sister. And I wonder if she felt the same way about saying good-bye to Tom and me.

Jim, the hospice nurse assigned to Lilly's case, kept saying that the young die harder than the old. During the final seven months, Lilly would become weak, unable to keep down any food and little water, seemed to be withdrawing, moving toward semi-consciousness. We would steel ourselves for the end. Then she would rally—weaker than before, yet alert, able to eat and interact with others. Naively, I thought these ups and downs were what Jim meant about the young dying harder. It wasn't until Lilly's last eleven days that the full meaning of his words sank in.

One of the small mercies of Lilly's particular form of cancer was the absence of prolonged, persistent, excruciating pain. This changed at 6:30 p.m. on Saturday, eleven days before she died. The pain that had plagued her intermittently suddenly spiked. It took 12 hours to bring it under control. Every day the pain seemed to break through and her pain medication was doubled and doubled again. Her bowel shut down; she couldn't eat; she could barely sip water through a straw; then suck it from a sponge held to her lips; then finally nothing. As her kidneys shut down and body wastes began to accumulate, she became more disoriented. Her breathing became increasingly ragged until moments of stillness were broken by huge, gasping gulps for air. This, I understood at last, was what Jim had meant. Each day, her suffering became more palpable. Still her body and mind and spirit would not give up. Jim, Maxie the wonderful personal care worker from hospice, a hospice volunteer, and a wise friend all began to ask Tom and me if we had given Lilly permission to let go and leave. Tom said he had, and I have no reason to doubt him. I said I had. In all honestly, however, my permission was oblique. "It's okay for you to be at peace," I would whisper. "Daddy's waiting to be with you. He loves you and will keep you safe." "It's okay not to fight anymore. You've fought so hard, you can rest now." I danced around the word "good-bye." I could not bring myself to say it; to say it was okay for her to go.

She fought so hard in those final days, beyond the point where it made any sense or served any meaningful purpose. Other than maybe she, too, could not bear to say "good-bye." Tom or I stayed close to Lilly's bedside; reading, dozing, working on our respective laptop computers. One or the other of us was in constant attendance. Maybe dying in our presence was too much a wrenching away, too explicit a leave-taking. Maybe in that quiet interlude between one dose of medicine and the next, in that brief time when Tom and I both drifted into sleep, she took her opportunity to slip unobtrusively away. I hope that this is so, that she did not feel I abandoned her at the end. I've heard anecdotes describing the same experience—a caregiver stepping from the room for a cup of coffee or to answer the phone, only to return a few minutes later to find their loved one gone. This offers some small comfort as I struggle with the ineffable lessons I began to learn at my sister's bedside.

I say *"began* to learn," because I associate actual learning with comprehension. At my sister's bedside, I came to see that some things are incomprehensible. I used to think I stood upon a scrap of ground from which I could comprehend the meaning of life. As surely as the grinding of tectonic plates fractures the earth's crust, my sister's struggle against the inexorable force of death fractured the ground beneath my illusions of comprehension.

In the mid-1950s, my parents finally succumbed to Lilly's and my pleas for a television, just in time for the golden age of the TV western. Lilly and I became instant addicts: *Rawhide, Bonanza, Wagon Train, The Lone Ranger, The Restless Gun, The Rebel, Laramie, The Big Valley, Zorro*, the list goes on and on. We would sit for hours, enthralled by the endless struggle between good and evil. It was so easy then, when the color of one's hat signaled from the outset who would win and who would lose. Perhaps being steeped in these frontier morality tales inculcated the belief that somehow, in spite of all odds, the good guys always win. No matter how dire the circumstances, no matter how hopeless the situation, the innocent are always rescued. If we live with integrity, courage, compassion, kindness, and courtesy; if we obey the rules; if we fulfill our obligations; if we are productive, responsible citizens of the universe, then we, too, will be saved in the end.

Throughout the four years of her illness and dying, Lilly exhibited a remarkable strength of character. She endured a series of experimental treatments, each one more invasive, more toxic, more potentially deadly. Time after time, she received the devastating news that the treatments had not arrested the spread of tumors, until finally, she had the courage to say, "no more," except for a course of radiation aimed at shrinking the tumors in her lungs. She did this in order to realize one last dream of taking our niece to Paris as a high school graduation gift.

Her zest for life persisted even as the circumference of her world shrank from Europe, to the United States, to Reno, to her house, to the recliner in her TV room, to her bed. Lilly loved good food and would recall with great enthusiasm the delicacies she had enjoyed in France. She husbanded her waning strength for outings to favorite Reno restaurants. When this was no longer possible, she waited with keen anticipation for a take-home dish that Tom and I would bring. When she could eat only three bites, or two, or one, she gave careful thought not just to which food might stay down, but which would yield the greatest pleasure. Toward the end, she was craving something cold and just a little sweet. Unable to find any Italian ice, I bought a frozen lemon fruit bar and cut off a tablespoon or two. She nibbled a bit of that and acted like I had brought her the finest feast this side of Julia Child's kitchen.

Lilly's passion for food was matched by her determination to remain productive. Her step-daughter was planning a trip to Paris in the spring that Lilly would not live to see. Surrounded by mounds of books, Lilly dictated travel notes, highlighted itineraries on maps, and expended her meager breath reassuring Sharon that she would be just fine managing the City of Lights on her own. Her friend Joyce, a musician and conductor of a community orchestra, wanted to adapt a children's tale to music. As the time for collaboration trickled away, Lilly decided to draft the story and identify suitable musical accompaniments. She was overwhelmed with gratitude when two friends came, recorded the story, and produced a demonstration CD.

Lilly claimed to be an introvert, but she had a capacity to connect with people through her sense of humor and keen intelligence. She looked forward to the visits from the hospice staff. She joked with Jim and Maxie, compared recipes, shared travel anecdotes, discussed politics and religion. Many times, Lilly would be drifting in a restless, twilight sleep, apparently too weak even to watch TV. Then a friend would telephone or stop by to say hello, and Lilly would rouse for an animated conversation, always about the visitor, never dwelling on herself. She was unflaggingly courteous, thanking well-wishers for flowers she could not bear to smell and goodies she could not bear to eat. For even the smallest of ministrations like fetching a fresh glass of water, fluffing her pillow, placing a cool compress on her forehead, Tom and I received a smile and a thank you.

As the management of her symptoms became more challenging, Lilly exercised considerable determination to maximize the benefit of her medications. Drugs to prevent coughing and constipation, caused nausea. Drugs to prevent nausea caused constipation. The hospice nurse would suggest different medications, or different formulations, or different dosage regimens. Initially, these changes seemed to have an adverse effect, but within a day or two Lilly would figure out an adjustment that would re-stabilize her condition for another few weeks. Instinctively, I would breathe a sigh of relief that the medications were working until it hit me that nothing was really working. This was no cure, only a temporary stay. Lilly's courage, generosity, productivity, respect, humor, compassion, kindness—none of these would restore her to life. There would be no last minute rescue. She was one of the good guys, and she was going to die before her rightful time. I've always thought it a bit of exaggeration when people say that some news took their breath away. But now I know it's true. Like a blow to the solar plexus, the finality of approaching death, in spite of all she had done right in her life, would leave me gasping for air and for consolation.

My parents, children of Italian immigrants bent on forging a better life for their families, valued hard work and education. They stressed the importance of learning and expected my sisters and me to lead lives of the mind. This isn't to say that physical activity, recreation, and fun were excluded. They were just subordinate to intellectual pursuits. Although my sisters and I were drawn to very different fields of study and professional endeavors, all three of us have a penchant for using our cognitive abilities to engage with the world and negotiate life's challenges. I had no cause to doubt the efficacy of this cerebral relationship with life until the final vigil at my sister's bedside.

The three physicians in my extended family had said that, all things considered, kidney failure is not a bad way to die. As waste products accumulate in the body, one lapses into sleep, then coma, then death. As Lilly's pain increased, as her lips dried and cracked from dehydration, as her rasping breaths became more ragged, I ached for Lilly to reach this state of peace and comfort. I would eye the bag where her dwindling output of urine accumulated, looking for some sign of impending release, then recoiling with guilt at this wish for death. "How can she keep producing urine when she's taking in so little?" I asked Jim in a hushed, kitchen conference. "It's a matter of balance between what she is taking in and putting out," he whispered back.

"Am I in balance?" Lilly began to ask. "Am I in balance?" At first I didn't grasp the import of the question as I held a moistened sponge to her lips. I simply murmured, "Yes."

"No! no!" she insisted impatiently. "Am I in balance? Am I taking in enough? Do I need more water?"

Shocked, I realized that somehow she had overheard Jim's comment. "Yes, you're in balance," I assured her.

"Don't patronize me. How much? How much do I need to be in balance?"

Stunned, I realized her mind was struggling to calculate the input, out-put ratio. In that moment, I faced the limits of cognition. Intelligence did not serve here. Education did not serve. Mental prowess did not serve.

"Your body is taking in as much as it can handle; it's putting out what it can. That means you're in balance," I explained.

"Is it enough; is it enough?"

As I tried fruitlessly to ease her mind, an impatient impulse flashed through me. "Just trust your body," I almost snapped. "It will do what it needs to." A wave of grief engulfed me. She couldn't trust her body. It had been invaded by enemy forces. It was literally failing her. What lay between a mind and body that no longer served? Spirit?

Lilly's semi-conscious wrestling with the equation of balance continued for a day or so as she moved slowly into a deeper, but hardly peaceful, sleep. Well beyond the last time when Lilly had taken in any fluid, urine continued to dribble through the catheter into the collection bag. "How can that be happening?" I asked Jim as I guiltily wrestled with desperation for it to be over and despair that it would be.

"She's young," Jim said, "and still has lots of tissue left. Her body is metabolizing that. It's the body's attempt to preserve itself."

`I stood by my sister's bed where only a few days earlier I had entertained the possibility of a human spirit suspended somewhere between or beyond mind and body. Was that spirit already gone, abandoning the body to this most primordial struggle for survival? Are we, in the final analysis, biological organisms instinctively driven to preserve the body, even at the cost of consuming it? I no longer harbor the illusion that I have answers to these questions. I no longer believe that cognitive capacities can ferret out the answers. I'm not sure that there are any answers on this side of the grave or on the other side.

This response is different, I assume, from those who approach life through their religious beliefs or capacity for spirituality. I've heard that some Catholic thinker once commented, "Give me a child to the age of five, and I will have him (or his mind) for life." Maybe the capacity for belief, for faith, is activated during those formative years. Recent studies of the brain show that various neural pathways are laid down at certain development stages. If the "programming" isn't completed during that critical window of opportunity, then it may never develop or may develop in a more stunted way. I no longer know whether it was a curse or a blessing that I slipped through the window of opportunity for the Catholic Church to instill its particular brand of spirituality and faith in my neurons.

As children, my sisters and I had no religious education. My parents, owners of a neighborhood pharmacy, worked seven days a week, including Sunday mornings. So, although we were baptized in the Catholic Church, we took no catechism classes. Attending mass occurred sporadically when one of my aunts would take us to Palm Sunday services at St. Phillips, a wonderfully mysterious stone church, filled with the aroma of incense, dappled light sifting through elaborate stained glass windows, the flickering glow of votive candles, and the burnished wood of the intricately carved confessionals. As a youngster, I was mesmerized by the ritualistic blessing with holy water, pew-side genuflections, and especially the offering of communion. The subliminal assimilation of such marvelous images, however, hardly sufficed as religious education. Nor did my mother's nightly recitation of the *Our Father* and *Hail Mary* at our bedsides.

I was a shy and socially awkward child with few friends. One afternoon—probably when I was in 6th or 7th grade—I was walking home from school when I heard a cluster of classmates talking excitedly about going to catechism at the nearby Presbyterian Church. Perhaps they asked if I were going, too. Perhaps they actually invited me to join them. Perhaps the idea of being part of this excited group tapped into an emergent adolescent need for belonging. For whatever reason, I ran home and asked my mother if I could go to catechism class. She was waiting on a customer at the candy counter, probably in the midst of ringing up a sale for a Snickers bar or newspaper, when she distractedly granted permission. So began my sojourn in the Presbyterian church, where in the span of four or five years I progressed from neophyte to an assistant youth Sunday school teacher.

Even then, during my infatuation with the idea of religion, the seeds of skepticism must have been germinating. Presbyterians in my community (maybe world-wide) were staunchly against the consumption of alcohol. One of the earliest demonstrable acts of belief was the signing of a temperance card, swearing that liquor would never pass my lips. Thus, my question was not well received. "If alcohol is so bad," I asked my elderly, timid Sunday school teacher one day, "why did Jesus turn water into wine?" Blushing, stammering, she ventured the notion, "Well, well—it really wasn't wine. It was grape juice."

As a freshman in college I attended the Presbyterian church conveniently located across the street from my dormitory. I was attracted by the titles of the sermons delivered by a minister who thought a bit more deeply about religious doctrine than my former Sunday school teacher. Then in my sophomore year I took an anthropology class in which the professor made a comment to the effect that cultures organized in tribal or clan units don't have a concept of monotheistic, hierarchical religion. In that instant, my belief, not only in organized religion, but in God, collapsed.

For some time I had been questioning the hypocrisy of religions that preach love and compassion, yet perpetrate acts of cruel intolerance. (And the absurdity of the water-to-grape juice doctrine still lingered.) I had assuaged those doubts by attributing religious hypocrisy and persecution to the fallibilities of self-serving humans who twist the "will of God" to their own evil purposes. But in hearing of this connection between social and religious structures, I suddenly realized that conceptions of God and spirituality are cultural constructs, artifacts of the human mind. No fatherly God is out there, orchestrating the universe for the benefit of our little speck of infinity. No omniscient being is running interference against life's vicissitudes; no ledger of good and bad deeds is being tallied in some cosmic accounting room. This realization did not precipitate a religious crisis. It simply catapulted me into a suspended state of disbelief—at times more atheistic; at times more agnostic.

I was 52 at the time Lilly's cancer was diagnosed. In the throes of mid-life reassessment, I had been trying to rid myself of what psychologist Robert Gerson calls "toxic anxiety." The antidote to this corrosive condition of perpetual free-floating fear seemed to be some sense of spirituality. I struggled against that pervasive image of a grandfatherly God with flowing white hair, beaming benignly on supplicant humans. There are, I reasoned, generative forces in the universe, forces that create and sustain life and health and beauty and good will on this earth. There are also forces of degeneration that destroy life and joy. Regardless of what does or does not come after this earthly existence, I can choose whether to align my smidgen of life-energy either with the generative or the degenerative forces of the universe. I bolstered this homespun existentialism with any anecdote that supported the notion of interconnected cosmic energy. Then Lilly received her death sentence.

Despite my own uncertainties, I struggled for ways to tap into some realm of spirituality, not for myself, but to benefit Lilly. Learning of scientific studies that demonstrated a positive relationship between prayer and healing, I put in a prayer request at St. Paul's Cathedral in Pittsburgh. Quite serendipitously, I met a Lubavitcher Rabbi who vouched for the efficacy of a particular intercessory prayer. Coupled with a contribution to a Jewish charity, the prayer was almost guaranteed to bring positive results he said with such fervent faith that I added this ritual to my incipient spiritual repertoire. Reading of spiritual energy that seems to transcend the artificial constructs of human time and space, I began to meditate, trying to channel generative energy toward Lilly. When none of this worked, I worried that my skepticism interfered with the transmission of any spiritual force. If only I could truly believe, then maybe Lilly would be cured. If only I knew how to ask, then maybe a cosmic rescue team would be deployed.

Both my sister and brother-in-law enjoyed music and played in community orchestras. Tom would often give a brief update on Lilly's condition at the weekly rehearsals and send her regards to the musicians. One night, a man approached Tom and began asking quite personal questions about Lilly's faith. Tom was taken aback at such presumption until the man identified himself as a Franciscan Brother. Father Art offered to come to the house and administer the sacrament of the anointing of the sick. Was this, at last, the eleventh hour rescue by the guys in the white hats?

Lilly and Tom conferred about Father Art's offer, and Lilly eventually agreed to see him. Apparently, she worried, as I did, about being a hypocrite, doubting the existence of God until we needed a miracle. I was not privy to the conversations in which Father Art assuaged her concerns, but I was present the second time he offered the sacrament, asking God to comfort Lilly and to give her courage, patience and hope.

Tom took great comfort in this prayer. I hope Lilly did as well. For me, it engendered rage. Lilly, it seemed to me, had already been coping with illness, pain, and impending death with courage, grace, and patience. The support of friends was immeasurable. God's blessing wasn't needed for any of this. What Lilly needed was the reward for being one of the good guys, the payoff for years of doing all the right things. She needed the restoration of her life. If this sacrament was not about balancing the cosmic ledger, then what was the point?

In the days following the anointing of the sick, a new desolation took root. For the first time, I could truly comprehend the choice of an amoral life. If there is no reward or punishment after death, then what does it matter how we live in the here and now? If selfishly taking whatever we want for ourselves has no eternal consequences, why not be greedy, profligate, indifferent to others? In the end, the guys with the white hats are just as dead as the guys in the black.

I suppose this accounts for the importance of faith; both faith in a life after death and faith in a final accounting for one's actions. I have no faith. Not long ago, *Time* magazine featured an article on life-after-death. Individuals who were revived from a documented state of clinical death (no heartbeat, no breathing, no brain waves), gave amazingly accurate and detailed descriptions of the medical action they had witnessed as the floated outside of their bodies. The article concluded that such evidence calls into question scientific assumptions about the boundary between life and death, the locus of human consciousness, and the presence of some "self" apart from the chemical pathways in our brains. Those of faith probably respond, "Of course!" But I, who am as skeptical of faith as I am of an anthropomorphic God with a white hat, say, "I just don't know…"

What I do know is that I am going to die. Perhaps this statement of the obvious may be forgiven in light of a human tendency to push the prospect of death to some distant horizon.

I was in my early 20s when I first experienced a general anesthetic. I remember lying on a gurney in a hospital hallway; the next thing I knew, I was waking up in a recovery room. Nothing in between. No dreams. No memories. No consciousness. No awareness of unconsciousness. Nothing. This, I thought, is what death is like.

One minute I'm here. The next I'm not, and I won't even know it. Since then, I've often wondered whether I would prefer to see death coming and take note of my last moment, or to just be gone. Lilly had chosen to know.

At the end of a check-up after a particularly rough few days, Jim sat beside Lilly and said, "You asked me to tell you when the end was coming. So far, I haven't said that to you. I've told you what will happen and general time frames, but I haven't said 'this is it.' I hadn't seen any signs that signaled the final stage. Today, I'm seeing those. If there are any people you want to see or be with, you should do that this weekend. I don't think it will be much longer."

After Jim left, Lilly took a deep breath and said, "Well, this takes some adjusting to. I mean you know it's out there, but somehow you forget. You think it's not going to be so close. That it won't come yet."

Even with death hovering by her bedside, the illusion of distance persisted. Even as I write, the illusion of distance is reasserting itself. But witnessing the death of my baby sister brought home the undeniable reality that I am going to die. If it has happened to Lilly, it will surely happen to me. And I will die alone.

By alone, I don't mean bereft of family and friends. I mean that I, like everyone else, will slip unaccompanied through that final passage. Again, this is not an astonishing revelation. It is a quiet, sobering truth, etched into my psyche by an acidic sense of helplessness. I wanted so desperately to save my sister; or if not to save her, to spare her from the repeated disappointments of unsuccessful treatments, from suffering, from fear, from loneliness, from eternal darkness. But I was helpless. Helpless to change the course of her illness. Helpless to forestall her dying. Waves of debilitating guilt washed through me. The breakfront against the swelling tide of guilt lay in the deepening existential realization that we are alone. Each of us. All of us. I could be present for my sister; I could have a presence in her life. But the journey of her life and death was hers alone. As is mine. So I know I am going to die, and I am going to die alone. In the meantime, all I can hope for is to be a loving presence in the lives of those I care about and have such loving presence grace my life.

Instinctively, I decided quite selfishly to spend as much time with Lilly as I could. If my presence could offer some comfort or diversion, if I could be of some help to Lilly and Tom, I was glad of that. But the bottom line was my need to be with her. We did not spend this time in deep conversations or emotional exchanges. We played *Scrabble* until it became too exhausting for Lilly to hold her head up to see the board. We watched the *Price is Right* each morning and *Jeopardy* each night. We watched innumerable home and garden shows—Lilly urging me to infuse more color into my conservative décor; waxing enthusiastic about Christopher Lowell's seven-layer approach to decorating; laughing in spite of the pain at my impression of the host of *Designing for the Sexes*. Other than *The West Wing,* we watched only sitcoms or the feel-good videos she dispatched me to rent. We culled her extensive collection of cookbooks—some for Tom, some for family, some for friends, the rest for a culinary program at the community college. We worked on Lilly's projects; sorted old family photographs; organized the extensive family history data she had been collecting; winnowed a lifetime of memorabilia. Always she smiled and thanked me. It was not enough. Most nights I cried with grief and guilt that neither my companionship nor my ministrations would save her. It was in these dark nights that I constructed the breakfront of existential aloneness.

It seems, however, a rather porous construction. Months after Lilly's death, the tide of guilt ebbs and flows. I find little joy in watching the TV shows we shared. Premieres of movies she wanted to see hold little interest. I breathe in the crisp air of crystalline autumn skies and breathe out tears of sadness for fall days she will never savor. Delicious meals, classical music, yard sales, vacation trips, walking a dog, news about mutual friends, loving embraces— such mundane pleasures, but pleasures she should have enjoyed into old age. Each reminder of all that she is missing releases fresh surges of guilt and grief. Perhaps in time, I can make the shift suggested by a wise psychologist and see myself as relishing life's little joys for

Lilly as well as myself. I know Lilly would want me to, but for now it feels like a callous disregard for all that she has lost.

I find some solace in my garden as I spread thick layers of mulch, as I till compost into heavy, sticky clay soil. I plant only trees, and shrubs, and flowers, perennials with their promise of vernal rebirth. I build a split-rail fence and stone walls. I dig post-holes for an arbor that Lilly and I envisioned together. As I work, my mind wanders. For brief interludes, I am released from the haunting pain over failing my sister.

When I express this sense of failure, friends are shocked and offer reassurance. "But you did so much for her; more than many others could or would do." Whether that is true or not, it offers little comfort, for in the end, that is where my failure lies. I wanted desperately to comfort Lilly, and anything I gave was dwarfed by the enormity of a death come too early and too hard to one of the good guys.

Jim had said that the final weeks could be a time of great spirituality, when Lilly and I could connect more deeply and meaningfully than ever. But there we were, watching *The Price is Right* and *Decorating Cents*. Where was the spirituality in that; where was the deep meaning; where was the comfort? I had squandered away the final months, weeks, days and, hours of our time together in frivolous pastimes. I had not risen above my own inhibitions about discussions of faith and death. I had offered no comfort to her spirit.

Maxie had suggested that Tom and I might pray with Lilly. When she had offered to do so, Lilly had accepted and seemed calmed by this shared act of faith. Praying aloud, praying with others, is a source of embarrassment to me. I can't quite figure out why an act that is supposed to be more meaningful when expressed within a community is embarrassing to me, but it is, just as talking about sex and money is. These are private, not public, matters.

As Lilly's final struggle became more palpable, I decided I should put my issues aside and try to pray with her. I mentally inventoried my meager knowledge of anything resembling a prayer and settled on the 23rd psalm. This, it seemed, might also serve as a way of saying good-bye, a way of giving permission to cross the valley of the shadow. Unbeknownst to me, Tom, too, must have taken Maxie's advice to heart and tried to pray with Lilly. When we talked later, it seemed we both had gotten a similar response. Upon hearing the first words of a prayer, Lilly startled out of a semi-conscious sleep, "What? What?" she asked in alarm. "What are you saying? What's going on?" Hardly the soothing response we had hoped for.

"Well," Tom said, "we really didn't have a relationship that included praying together. Some couples do, but that wasn't part of our life together."

Nor had it been part of Lilly's and my relationship.

We spent our final time together holding true to the lifelong patterns of relationship. Ours was a relationship of affection and companionship, formed in early years on the playground, roaming the woods behind our elementary school, watching those westerns and absorbing lessons of right and wrong. Within the constricting sphere of her dwindling life, Lilly found ways to hold on to the pleasures she valued. Within the constricting span of our final time together, we found ways to hold on to the pleasures we had always shared. No grand gestures. No infusion of cosmic grace or spiritual intimacy. Just small comforts. Insignificant in the face of eternal loss. Yet beyond measure of love between sisters knitting the unraveling threads of our lives together into final memory.

2

Circling in an Eddy of Grief

Like a battered branch circling in a swirl of river water, I am floating in an eddy of grief. When the image of an eddy first came to mind, I asked my husband, a mechanical engineer specializing in fluid flow, to explain the dynamics of this phenomenon. From what I could understand of his explanation, it seems that when water encounters an obstacle and flows around it, the pressure is inevitably greater on one side of the obstacle than on the other. This differential in pressure pulls the water into a circular motion, thereby creating an eddy. Like submerged river rock, the illness and death of my younger sister, Lilly, disturbed the placid flow of my life, creating differences in pressure that propel me in circles. It would be easier in some ways to move on with my life, to progress through the stages of grief so neatly outlined in the psychology texts. Yet, I am content to linger for a time in my existential eddy to see what meanings might emerge as I contemplate this loss.

Not long ago, I heard a clinical psychologist speak about his work with families on a children's cancer unit. Dr. P, as I will call him, talked about wanting to find a way to shorten the time it takes for parents to move through their grief and depression. As I watched him sketch out the points of grief on the chalk board and stab impatiently at the gap between where parents are and where he thinks they should be, I could feel outrage welling up within me. "What gives him the right," I thought, "to say how long it should take parents to get through their grief about such a horrific experience?"

This question itself creates a pressure differential that keeps me swirling in my eddy. As wrenching as it was to watch my sister's losing battle with cancer, I can barely imagine the agony of witnessing this struggle in one's child. Perhaps Dr. P sees parents caught, not in a placid eddy, but in a violent whirlpool of anxiety, fear, grief, and depression. In imminent danger of drowning, these parents may need a lifeline to pull them into safer, more navigable currents. With this image, I can empathize with the psychologist's desire to expedite movement through a process of grieving. I can also understand the urgency of this desire when other children in the family need the love and attention of grieving parents.

That said, however, I still struggle with another facet of my outrage engendered, not by his desire to offer clinical help to these stressed families, but by his assumption about how to determine what constitutes effective help. Just as many streams flow together to form a river, the flow of my life is constituted from intermingling identities. Not only am I a grieving sister, I am also an educator and a researcher. In expressing his desire to find an answer to help his clients, Dr. P was dismissive of the type of qualitative research I value. "There is no good, <u>scientific</u> research that <u>proves</u> what we should do to help such clients," he asserted. "Sure, there are lots of books in the stores, but they are just people's stories. They are not based on sound research." This comment reflects assumptions about the nature of legitimate research that have dominated western thinking since the Enlightenment. For centuries, these assumptions have created an ontological vortex drawing into its powerful current everything that surrounds it.

I do not need the likes of this psychologist to pull me expeditiously from the eddy of my grief. What I do need is a lifeline to keep me from being sucked to the bottom of a whirlpool of science where my individuality, where my life experience, where the narrative meanings of my existence are of no consequence. For at the heart of Dr. P's criticisms of personal accounts lies a view of "real," scientific research that is interested in pinpointing exactly the type of lifeline that can pull grieving people from the whirlpool. In the quest for the ultimately effective lifeline, the specifics of my grief and my sister's dying don't matter. I want to scream out in protest, "I do matter. My sister mattered. The experiences of those terrified and grieving parents matter. How dare you ignore us in your quest for some scientifically validated lifeline? How dare you assume that the best thing you can do for us is to drag us efficiently out of living our experience of loss into some normalized place of post-grief?"

Having screamed this silent protest, however, I feel a different pressure exert itself and once again I am propelled around the eddy. This pressure is a longing for scientific certainty that I share with Dr. P. I wanted Lilly's physicians to have answers, not just any answers, but the right answers. I wanted to hear confident declarations that, "We know how to fix this." Whatever longings for scientific certainty Dr. P might harbor pale to insignificance in comparison to my aching desire for clear, predictable knowledge that would have restored Lilly to health. The cruel irony, of course, was that the only biomedical certainty available was the 95% probability that she would be dead within five years.

In a valiant effort to tip the odds even slightly in her favor, Lilly entered into a clinical trial that was testing an immunotherapy for kidney cancer. When you stop to think about it, kidney cells have to be very tough, otherwise they would be damaged as they filter waste products from the body. Normally, this toughness is a good thing, but it creates a virtually insurmountable problem when trying to eradicate kidney cancer. Chemotherapy and radiation—the big guns in the medical arsenal against many other cancers—just aren't that effective against kidney cancer. So the idea of immunotherapy is to enhance the body's own mechanisms for destroying the aberrant cells. The clinical trial that Lilly entered used Interleukin-2 to boost cancer fighting T-cells. At least that was the theory being tested in a protocol that consisted of three infusions of high-dose Interleukin-2 a day for seven days and then two weeks off before the cycle was repeated another seven times. After enough patients had completed this protocol, the researchers would be able to say with a reliable degree of certainty whether this treatment did or did not work. Now THIS is the type of SCIENTIFIC research that the clinical psychologist wants to bring to bear on the "treatment" of grief. This valid research would go beyond the merely anecdotal accounts of death, dying, and grief in the books on the shelves of Barnes and Noble. This type of research would yield more valuable results than observations coming from his years of experience in working with families caught in the virulent whirlpool of grief. And, if I were sitting on my doctor's exam table in a flimsy disposable gown waiting to learn whether I had cancer, I, too, would want valid and reliable scientific research proving the efficacy of a particular treatment.

But here is the problem. High-dose Interleukin-2 is so toxic that virtually no one enrolled in the clinical trial had ever completed the entire eight-cycle protocol. Nor had they necessarily received the full dose of Interleukin-2 during the week of 21 infusions that were administered in an intensive care unit so that specially trained nurses could watch for the warning signs of imminent brain hemorrhage or cardiac arrest. Among the patients enduring this regimen, one particularly strong young woman had attained legendary status for having come closer to meeting the ideal protocol than anyone else. She died before Lilly.

Let me be clear. I am not negating the importance of this clinical research or the value of the information that comes from the enormous suffering and courage of the individuals who participate in it. My point is simply this—let us be honest about the alleged precision and objectivity of "real/scientific" research.

The reality of the clinical trial lay not in the ideal protocol, but in the willingness and capacity of individuals to endure it. The physician researcher could record dosage levels and schedules for each patient. He could record all sorts of demographic data (age, marital status, level of education, work history, number of children, family history of cancer); physiological measures (blood pressure, pulse, respiration, red blood cell count, T-cell levels), and reactions to the Interleukin-2 (nausea, hallucinations, shivering tremors so violent that a hospital bed begins to vibrate across the room). What cannot be measured are the ineffable qualities that allow someone to enter into and stay the course of treatment. Is it so great a fear of death that the rigors of treatment are of lesser consequence? Is it a zest for life or a yet-to-be accomplished goal that makes the gamble worthwhile? Is it a desire to give meaning to one's illness and probable death by contributing to the understanding of cancer treatment? Is it a variation in physical or psychological tolerance to pain? What imaginable and unimaginable well-springs of fortitude come into play when life-threatening illness disrupts the flow of one's existence?

So as I float in my eddy of grief, here is what I would like to say to Dr. P. Life threatening illness precipitates an existential crisis. It strips away the comforting diversions of ordinary life that allow us to push the prospect of death to the periphery of awareness. Each of us is going to respond to the prospect of our own mortality or the mortality of those we love in very individual and personal ways. What I want in that moment of existential angst is not a scientific cure for my grief. I want compassion and understanding. I want for others to see me, to see my sister. The power of this desire to be seen seems especially potent when the specter of annihilation hovers at my shoulder.

In recounting his experiences on the cancer unit, Dr. P mentioned that a number of parents have asked him to be present when the failure of biomedical science has brought their child to the moment of death. This suggests to me that he already brings a wisdom and compassion to his work with grieving parents. If not, why would they include him in this most intimate experience? Has Dr. P been sucked so far down into the vortex of rationalistic scientific research that he can place no credence in the wisdom that already lies within his own heart?

If I am content to circle for a time in an eddy of grief, what purpose is served by measuring that choice against some standard protocol for "normal" mourning? I was appalled not long ago when I realized I had not thought of Lilly throughout my busy day. I had shed no tears for her. As the two year anniversary of her death approaches, does this mean I am moving toward a healthier psychological space or have I already branded myself as pathologically depressed—a victim of traumatic grief—because I want to shed tears for Lilly "so long" after she is gone?

What do my tears represent? A failure to grieve efficiently? A failure to achieve a stage of acceptance or resolution? A failure to seek psychological help? A failure of scientific research to provide a sturdy lifeline as I swirl in my eddy of existential grief? In the end, what matters? An understandable, yet unattainable, quest for pristine scientific knowledge or a compassionate empathy for our strivings to live and to love in the shadow of soul wrenching loss?

When Lilly died, her husband Tom sent a note to the staff of the hospital where she had completed as much of the clinical protocol as she could endure. In the end, the physician-scientist-researcher who ran the clinical trial had had no magic lifeline to throw her. What he did have, upon hearing of Lilly's death, was an expression of sympathy for Tom's loss. I will not speak for Tom, but for me it matters that this researcher saw Lilly as more than an anonymous subject, more than a set of data points in a less than perfect scientific experiment. His acknowledgement of her passing and of Tom's loss is no sturdy rope of salvation. It is a gossamer thread of human connection. When scientific knowledge fails, as it inevitably does, to fulfill its promise of immortality, the intertwining of these gossamer threads is all that may keep us afloat in the streams and eddies of our lives.

3

Coming Face to Face with Death

I did not grow up in what I imagine to be a typical (perhaps stereotypical) Italian American family—a large, multigenerational, extended family living within a close-knit ethnic community. There was no yearly succession of celebrations to attend—weddings, baby showers, baptisms, confirmations, birthdays, anniversaries, and funerals—as grandparents, parents, aunts, uncles, cousins, brothers, sisters, and neighbors moved through life's momentous passages. I do not carry with me a repertoire of social, cultural, or familial rituals for marking such occasions. As a child, I did not learn how to sit with death. I did not learn how to be with the dying. Indeed, as a child, I was sheltered from death.

All of my grandparents were already dead, well before I was born, except for a step-grandmother who died when I was 5 or 6 years old. I did not attend her funeral; not the visitation; not the mass; not the burial. The same held true when one of my aunts and one of my uncles died. Even then, I sensed my parents' desire to shield me from this mysterious, painful presence. So, although they alluded to these deaths, the face of death was always "off stage," a shadow lurking in the wings.

When I was in college, another aunt was stricken with cancer. My parents seemed to have no expectation that I would visit her in the hospital. Again, that desire to shelter, to protect. In what may well have been my first act of independent adulthood, I figured out how to reach the hospital via public transportation and saw my aunt shortly before she died. I do not recall if I went to her funeral. I think I must have, but only faint memories linger. More vivid is my recollection of wanting to keep my trip to the hospital from my mother. I knew she would not be happy with my night-time adventure from the eastern to northern suburbs of Pittsburgh, a journey requiring transfers to three different buses at some of the seamier corners of our fair city.

In more recent years, as I pay my respects to friends who have lost a loved one, I am always struck by the presence of children at the funeral home. Often dressed in their Sunday best, they wander among the crowd, entertaining themselves, occasionally seeking attention from grown-ups, sometimes boisterous, sometimes subdued. In their wanderings, they brush past the casket where the cosmetic face of death is center stage. Does this early introduction, I wonder, make the raw face of death less startling, less strange?

I have seen this raw face only twice. The first was my father's and I did not understand what I was seeing. My father was admitted to the hospital on the night of April 1, a cruel April fool's joke on a night meant for love and celebration. That evening we had attended the wedding reception of a close friend. As the festivities waned, my future husband and I stole away surreptitiously to enjoy a much anticipated night's dalliance. The next morning I learned my father had begun his two week dance with death. Accompanied by the beat of medical monitors, the dance spun wildly through an intricate choreography of arrhythmias, cardiac arrests, and resuscitations. My mother, my sisters, and I were helpless spectators, not knowing, in any moment, whether to hope or to despair. In the early morning hours of April 15, my mother called me to the hospital. I rushed to the room, saw my father lying in bed, and felt a flood of relief, of joy. "He's better," I thought. "He doesn't need the wires and tubes and monitors. He's okay." Then I took in his open mouth; the backward tilt of his head; the incredible stillness of his face; my mother's mournful vigil. In that moment, at the belated age of 31, I came face to face with death. Twining through my grief was shame at my foolish, ill-founded joy. When I saw the face of death, I did not know it.

I thought I would be better prepared the second time.

"Maria…Maria…" The hushed voice of my brother-in-law roused me from a restless sleep. "I think she's gone."

Even as I pushed aside the remnants of troubled dreams, the dread seeped down through my chest into my stomach. Steeling myself, I padded softly behind Tom toward the bedroom where my sister had lain dying for over four months.

"I gave her medicine at 9:00," Tom whispered. "And set the alarm for midnight. For the next dose. But I woke up a few minutes ago. I don't think she's breathing."

Such tentativeness, such hesitancy from this normally take-charge kind of guy. I felt the flutter of anxiety brush against my heart. The irrational thought, "But he's the grown up. How will I know if he doesn't?"

We tiptoed to a stop. "She looks like a bird," I thought with a shock. Lilly lay on her back as she had since conceding that the hospice bed would be more practical than her own. Her face was turned toward the right; her head tilted back and up, her mouth open—like a baby bird's grasping for food. Her nose looked sharper with a beakish quality accentuated by sunken cheeks. Her eyes, open and glassy. Wisps of disheveled hair haloed her head like a feathered crown. And the indelible stillness.

This bird-like image is the second face of death etched into memory. I was no more prepared for it than the first. Perhaps these still-life portraits simply accumulate, forming a collage, not of preparation, but of remembrance.

4

On the Death of a Sister

Intellectually, I know that death can visit any of us at any time. None of us is guaranteed our three score and ten years. Still, emotionally, I had clung to the comforting illusion that death lurked on some distant horizon for me and those I love. My younger sister's diagnosis not only shattered that illusion; it finally brought home to me the shadow of death that had hovered near my mother throughout her life.

When my mother spoke of her family of origin, it was a recitation of deaths. I walled myself off from the litany, sensing some particular response was expected, but never knowing what it should be. I was especially irritated when Mom mentioned her sister, Linda, who had died of tuberculosis around age 22. I had never known this person. What was the point of announcing the date of her birth or the fact that she had died? I already knew this information. I could see no purpose in the periodic repetition of these isolated details. In the instant of Lilly's death sentence, I finally understood.

Mom was only a year or so younger than her sister Linda. They were childhood companions, just as Lilly and I had been. Together they endured the hardships of poverty, the horror of war, the pain of never quite fitting in. The prospect of losing my sister was intolerable. How intolerable it must have been for my mother to lose a sister who, I suspect, had been the sole source of social and emotional support during her lonely and frightened childhood.

Lilly was our family genealogist. During her months of dying we sorted through the boxes of family artifacts she had accumulated. Nestled among stacks of musty postcards was a letter that Linda had written to her family from a sanatorium in the mountains of Italy. Apparently a priest had persuaded her that this form of quarantine was a wise course of action. When I asked an uncle what he remembered about Linda's leaving for Italy, he said it happened rather quickly. I had the impression that there had been no good-byes. Perhaps this was to protect the rest of the family from potential infection.

Since reading Linda's letter, I have been haunted by the image of a beautiful, vital young woman being wrenched away from family and friends and dying alone in a foreign country. I wonder now if that image haunted my mother as well. Mingling with the grief for my sister's too-early death is now a muted grief for my mother's sister who never had a chance for love, marriage, children. What sorrows, fears, and longings kept a vigil by her deathbed?

My sister Linda is named after my mother's sister. I have always known this fact. Now I understand the need to keep alive a memory, to honor a loved one, to create even the smallest of legacies. Lilly, dying at 54, had had a chance to establish a presence among family and friends, within her professional and social communities. She is remembered. In restating the fact of her sister Linda's birth and death, my mother may simply have been giving witness to a life that had ended too soon. The only response that may have been expected from me was to pause for a moment of remembrance.

Lilly's terminal illness created the potential for an emotional connection between my mother and me. But my sisters and I wanted to spare my mother the pain of losing her youngest child. As Lilly was waging her four-year battle with cancer, my mother was passing from the early to middle stage of Alzheimer's disease. By the time Lilly knew the battle was lost and shared this with our mother, the memory of this devastating information faded away within an hour. I did not bring it back. The bond of losing a sister lay in my heart but not between my mother and me.

Too late I came to a place where I was able to voice the questions that I should have asked my mother years ago. What was Linda like? What would you like me to know about her, to remember? How did her death affect you? Too late, I came to a place where I might be able to bear hearing my mother's grief.

They say long-term memory goes after short-term memory. As Alzheimer's disease strips away the present, the past becomes more immediate. I wondered if my mother, even in her greatly diminished state, could still speak of her sister. I asked her, "Can you tell me about your sister Linda?"

"She died."

"What happened to her?

A long pause. A searching back through shredded neural pathways. "It was something she ate, I think."

"Oh. That's sad." I let the memory fragment recede. Now I grieve the loss of both sisters—hers and mine, gone way before their time.

5

I Kill Earthworms

I kill earthworms. Not intentionally. Not with malice. But regretfully. They are hapless collateral casualties in my war on weeds and my efforts at garden building. When I am stabbing at dandelion roots or digging mulch into the soil, I inevitably sever these poor, unsuspecting creatures. When the cruel blow is not instantaneously fatal, they curl convulsively or wriggle frantically to escape. I wonder in those moments about their desire to live and at the vagaries of fate. The double-pronged weeder misses one worm and slays another. The shovel edge slices some and spares others. Often, when I'm not too tired, I bend over and move these friends of the soil out of harm's way. Then I wonder at unseen forces that so capriciously dispense death or salvation.

The earthworms are minding their own business, going about their tasks of daily living. In an instant, without forewarning, pain is inflicted, life is terminated. So it is with us. Recently I heard a news story about a plane crash; 43 passengers died; one boy survived. Was God too tired to reach down and save more than one? Or, as some suggest, is there a greater plan being served; God with a grand garden design in which some of us are regrettable collateral damage?

Sometimes as I'm toiling away in the hot sun with flies buzzing around my sweat-covered face, I consider abandoning the whole gardening project. There are just too many noxious weeds. No matter how hard I work, they are always popping back up. The good plants seem too few and far apart. They seem to grow so much slower than their aggressive counterparts. I'm reminded of the world weary, father-god in *The Children of Eden*. Try as he might to cultivate the good, the bad always insinuates itself till he wants to wash his hands of the whole human enterprise. Is that it, then? Has God gone off to put his feet up, have a cool drink, and leave us to thrive or perish as best we can?

Or is there something a bit more sinister at play? Obedience and disobedience. A father-god who smiles with favor upon his compliant children, rewarding their fidelity to his seemingly arbitrary dictates. Those who doubt, those who transgress his mandates, get hit with the cosmic shovel. This could be reassuring. Except for one small detail. From my humble perspective, it often seems that rewards and punishments rain down upon us as arbitrarily as my gardening kills or spares earthworms.

I feel sorry for the earthworms whose lives are so abruptly terminated. If I had the time and energy, I'd move them all to safety. I derive no pleasure from inflicting death upon such lowly creatures. How can I, a flawed human being, feel more compassion than a God who is touted to be loving and omnipotent? Wouldn't such an august being want to spare us lowly human life forms? The pragmatic response is that death is part of life. The old must give way to make room for the new. We, as much as the earthworms, are part of these natural cycles. Which brings me full circle to the capriciousness of it all. Just as earthworms live or die on a whim, so apparently, do we. A news report told of a mother and child swept by a flash flood into a raging river. Just as the mother was about to lose consciousness, her hair caught on a branch. The pain roused her, and she clung to the tree until rescued. The dice rolled in her favor that day. The dice rolled against my sister. She gets cancer and dies at 54. I am spared—at least for now. What do I make of that? What do I make of my life? What, in the end, does it really matter?

6

On the Edge

Several years before my sister's death, her husband asked my mother, "Lillian, what are your happiest memories?" I cringed as my mother launched into a long familiar patchwork of misery, whose chronology I could never quite discern. Sailing for days in steerage—once to America; once back to Italy. Grinding poverty on both sides of the Atlantic. Walking in the bitter cold along railroad tracks in Boston, picking up bits of coal that had fallen from passing trains. Walking in the bitter cold, wind-swept mountains of Italy, scrounging twigs and bits of wood for the stove. Ridiculed by American classmates for speaking Italian; ridiculed by Italian classmates for dressing like *una Americana*. Always the outsider. Waving to soldiers guarding an armory as she went to school one morning in war-torn Italy; seeing only spatters of red on the wall where they had stood when she returned home that afternoon. A nighttime exodus from the tiny, three floor walk-up apartment, through the high mountain passes outside of Brescia, one step ahead of the fascist police. The omni-present sense of danger. "Get an education," was the family motto. "What you have up here," a touch to the forehead, "they can never take away." The unremitting threat of the unnamed "they." For as long as I can remember, the memories were shared with an intensity of hysteria and horror as if they had just occurred.

One weekend, during a personal growth workshop, I shared this crazy quilt account of my mother's story. One of the participants was a Jewish psychiatrist. As a teenager, he had used considerable cunning and daring to elude Hitler's troops, first in Germany, then in Poland. During a break, he came up to me and said, "The way you talk, the way you think, it's as though you're a war refugee." At that moment, I understood how fully, how completely, I had absorbed my mother's pervasive sense of dread.

This dread permeated her parenting style. She cautioned me against reckless living, never failing to point out examples of the deadly consequences of risky behavior. The bicycle rider smashing into a telephone pole and dying. A horseback rider falling and lying paralyzed from the neck down. No activity was too mundane or innocuous to be free of potentially catastrophic consequences. As an adult, I recognize these admonitions as my mother's attempt to keep me safe. One would think I could shed this cloak of catastrophic thinking. In so many ways I have been blessed—with good health, good fortune, good friends, a good marriage, a good education. Yet, I am always braced for unexpected catastrophe. When my husband goes out for a day of road biking or skiing, I steel myself for the possibility that I may be a widow by evening.

On the corner of Fifth Avenue and Smithfield Street, across from Pittsburgh's iconic Kaufmann's Clock, a steady stream of Port Authority buses chugs past, spewing acrid pollution into the air. Whenever I pause at this intersection to wait for the light to change, I think of Sam Hood. Perhaps he was reading the evening edition of *The Pittsburgh Press* for which he was a columnist. That detail I'll never know; nor what caused the driver to lose control of his bus and smash into Sam more than 60 years ago. I could not have been older than 10 when the death of this family friend was the first catastrophic story I collected in my own right.

Over the years, I've added celebration-turned-to-tragedy vignettes to my collection. Whenever I drive past the runaway truck sand pile just before the west-side entrance of The Fort Pitt Tunnel, I glance in my rear view mirror. Good! No tractor trailers barreling out of control down Greentree Hill. I flash back to the semi that actually made it through the tunnel, across the bridge, and onto Stanwix Street—obliterating a family before screeching to a halt near the long-gone Jenkins Arcade. The family had come to Pittsburgh to celebrate a daughter's college graduation.

On July 9, 2003, just north of Pittsburgh, a trucker ran a stop sign and collided with a car having the right-of-way on Rt. 8. A North Carolina family of five on an outing to Moraine State Park died in the fiery crash. I can no longer nap in the car on those rare occasions when I reluctantly relinquish control of driving to my husband. What if we have the misfortune to be in such a crash? I'd never know what had happened.

This horror of being gone in an unknowing instant is exacerbated by images of dying in prolonged moments of terror. Like a slow-growing parasite, this anxiety has been nurtured by accounts of airplane crashes. Each time I am faced with a mid-travel change of itinerary, I think of the businessman whose meetings finished early, allowing him to switch his reservation to U.S. Airways Flight 427 which crashed in a field outside of Pittsburgh on a beautiful September evening in 1994. As I descend into the Fort Lauderdale airport, I think of the ValuJet that slammed into the viscous mud of the Everglades. As I board a plane to Europe, I recall the TWA New York-to-Paris flight that exploded over the Atlantic, killing a former colleague, her husband, and granddaughter on their way to a special vacation to Europe.

A shooting spree several years ago in Wilkinsburg punctured any illusion that staying close to home offers some safety from unexpected, tragic death. My husband regularly visited a property adjacent to a McDonald's where a man was shot as he waited in his car. With a shudder, I think of the number of times I have waited for my husband in that same parking lot. When I pass construction sites where giant cranes loom over the road, I think of my friend's son who died at his desk when such a crane crashed through the window of his living room. I read of a Good Samaritan who stopped to help a victim of domestic violence and was shot dead.

These events have etched into my psyche an awareness of just how fragile life is. I wish I could say that this awareness has, in turn, engendered a desire to live each moment to the fullest. This is, unfortunately, not the case. Years ago, a friend and colleague invited me to consult on a project in war-torn Bosnia. I turned her down, joking that "I am one bad hair day away from full-scale agoraphobia." Sadly, this is much less a joke than I wish it were.

Not long ago, a friend who is also prone to catastrophic thinking suggested that I might use meditation, relaxation exercises or deep breathing to purge my feelings of anxiety. Failing that, a nice anti-anxiety medication might do the trick. These are entirely reasonable antidotes, except for one small detail. My mother's hyper-vigilance seems to be encoded in my DNA. If the toxic coding were sucked from my genes, if my neural pathways were cleansed of anxiety, what would fill these spaces? Joy? Okay. Spontaneity? Acceptable, maybe. A sense of adventurous abandon? Not so acceptable. Daring risk-taking? Definitely NOT OKAY.

Early in the summer of 1999, I was reading Robert Gerzon's book, *Finding Serenity in the Age of Anxiety*. I chided myself for my catastrophic way of being. "Enough is enough," I thought. "Really, everything is good. Life is good. Just relax. Accept your good fortune. Embrace joy. Be grateful." Others would, I am sure, view this as a long overdue step away from the edge of neurosis.

That September, Lilly was diagnosed with terminal cancer.

7

Shopping for Steak
at Home Depot

Let me begin my reflection with a disclaimer—I am not seriously, chronically, or terminally ill. This, I believe, colors my response to Havi Carel's book, *Illness: The Cry of the Flesh*. Despite my good health, I resonate deeply with the following passage in which Carel argues for the benefits that might be derived by approaching illness from a phenomenological perspective:

> It could improve the patient-clinician relationship by being an antidote to the objectification and alienation so many patients complain of. In the past two years I have had daily contact with other patients from the UK as well as other Western countries. The complaint that seems to appear near-universal in this context is this: why am I not treated as a person? This complaint points to a certain culture within the medical world, of treating disease as a purely biological dysfunction. If disease is seen as a malfunction of a body part it (and the ill person) will be treated very differently than if

it is seen as a world-transforming event, modifying the life-world of the ill person. A phenomenological approach would introduce this missing first-person perspective on illness and would enable health professionals to understand the transformation of the world of the ill person caused by the illness.[2]

I share Carel's belief that understanding illness from a first person perspective would lead to a different type of clinician-patient relationship. Several weeks after reading Carel's book, however, I had an epiphany; expecting clinicians to be responsive to the existential transformations precipitated by catastrophic illness is like shopping for steak at Home Depot. The following recollections trace events that led to this jaundiced, yet liberating, perspective.

Although I did not have Carel's language of phenomenology, when I was a child of 10 or 11, I felt intuitively that something was amiss in the medical world. At the time, one of my uncles was dying from cancer. Back then, children were not allowed to visit the hospital and my parents did not talk with my sisters or me about his illness. I just caught whiffs of the experience—his determination to fight, the sadness surrounding his decline, the sorrow for his death. This was, I think, the first intimation that better, more open communication was needed.

Years later, this intimation grew clearer and stronger when the father of my best friend suffered a heart attack. It appeared he had recovered, but then he died suddenly a week or so after being discharged from the hospital. He had been carrying sheets of wood paneling up a set of stairs when he collapsed. His last, barely coherent words in the ambulance were, "I've got to get to work." He had been a bus driver. With a heart condition, it was likely that he would never have returned to work. I wondered if this had been preying on him and that at some level he had precipitated his second and fatal attack by tackling a physical chore far beyond the capacity

---

2   Havi Carel, *Illness: The Art of Living*, 44-45.

of his damaged and still healing heart. "Someone should have talked with him," I thought. "There should have been someone to find out how he was feeling emotionally—not just physically. There should have been counseling." Now, of course, decades later, a whole sub-industry of cardiac rehabilitation has been established within the medical world. But at that time, patients were released on their own recognizance.

This belief that someone "should have talked with him," eventually led me to the idea expressed by Carel: health care clinicians should be trained to talk with patients, to understand what they are going through, to help them to respond with empathy in the face of cataclysmic illness. This was not, of course, an original idea. Several years before my friend's father died, Elizabeth Kübler-Ross had expressed the same view in her landmark book, *On Death and Dying; What the Dying have to Teach Doctors, Nurses, Clergy, and Their Own Families*. Unfortunately, in a medical world driven by diagnosis and treatment, Kübler-Ross' concept of "stages" quickly became a gauge for measuring whether patients (and by extension their loved ones) were grieving "properly." Apparently the import of the book's subtitle was lost upon those looking for what they should do to patients rather than ways of being with patients.

Interestingly, more than 40 years after the publication of *On Death and Dying*, physician-author Atul Gwande expressed many of the same concerns in his best selling book, *Being Mortal: Medicine and What Matters in the End*. In 2016, physician Paul Kalanithi added his voice to the call for empathy in his memoir, *When Breath Becomes Air*. What should we make of these recurring calls for "empathy training" despite the efforts of many medical schools to incorporate courses on topics of "patient-physician relations," "death and dying," "the healing power of narrative," "communication skills," and "the human/social side of medicine?"

Gwande offers an insight into the situation as he recounts his own medical school exposure to Tolstoy's *Death of Ivan Ilyich* in a course on ethics:

What worried us [medical students] was knowledge.
While we knew how to sympathize, we weren't at all
certain we would know how to properly diagnose and
treat. We paid our medical tuition to learn about the
inner process of the body, the intricate mechanisms of
its pathologies, and the vast trove of discoveries and
technologies that have accumulated to stop them. We
didn't imagine we needed to think about much else.
So we put Ivan Ilyich out of our heads.[3]

Truth be told, if I am sick, I want a physician who has pursued
knowledge as ferociously as Gwande. I want someone with the
knowledge to cure me. While empathy would be nice, I can live
(quite literally) without being "treated as a person." But if I were
in Carel's situation—facing an incurable, chronic, degenerative,
terminal illness—then what is the nature of help I would desire? My
assumption, like Carel's, is that I deserve to be treated as a suffering
human being in need of social, emotional, spiritual support as well
as medical treatment. For decades I harbored a sense of outrage that
clinicians would not respond humanely to these deeper existential
needs of their seriously and critically ill patients.

Then, several weeks after reading Carel's book, I read *At the
Will of the Body: Reflections on Illness* by Arthur Frank in which
he contrasts his experience of a heart attack with his diagnosis of
testicular cancer. Of the heart attack from which he fully recovered,
he writes:

I was more than willing to define what had happened
as what medicine calls an "incident." It was a flat tire
on the road of life, an annoying but minor breakdown.
Some time had been lost, I had gotten a little dirty
while repairs were made, but the tire was patched

---

3   Atul Gwanda, *Being Mortal: Medicine and What Matters in the End.*

and I could continue the journey as if nothing had happened.[4]

In contrast, he compares receiving a diagnosis of cancer to having his life ripped up, like a street near his home that is jack hammered every year to address some new problem. He explains:

> After an incident like my heart attack I was able to bounce back. People even said, "You've really bounced back." That's accurate, because most cases we do not sink into an experience, we only hit the surface. I may have bounced back from a heart attack, but with cancer I was going to have to sink all the way through and discover a life on the other side. Cancer was not going to be an incident; I would have to experience it.[5]

Frank goes on to detail his struggle to experience cancer and sink through that experience to a new existential reality. Like Carel, he wants to be treated as a person, not simply as a disease. Yet, as he says, "Most medical staff do not have the time to be caregivers, and many may not have the inclination. They provide treatment, which is no less important than caregiving, but it is not at all the same." [6]

Caring, Frank contends, is discerning the particularities of each person's experience of disease and responding to what that individual needs to cope with the existential consequences of those particularities. Treatment, on the other hand, is the application of a predetermined recipe to an identifiable category of physiological dysfunction. When the dysfunction is a temporary incident, the medical establishment arrives like the Automobile Association to

---

4   Arthur W. Frank, *At the Will of the Body*, 19.

5   Arthur Frank, p. 28

6   Arthur Frank, p. 49.

fix a flat tire on one's life journey. But when the dysfunction is fundamentally unfixable, it triggers the medical establishment's

> ...belief that unless they can do something to reduce the bodily suffering, they have failed as professionals. Continuing suffering threatens them, so they deny it exists. *What they cannot treat, the patient is not allowed to experience.* [7](emphasis added)

As Carel and Frank point out, the medical world is rife with subtle and not-so-subtle signals prohibiting the expression of one's existential angst over life-threatening, life-altering illness. For years, I wanted medical personnel to change (to become enlightened) so that the prohibitions would be lifted, and it would be possible to talk about one's fears. Like Carel, I wanted health care personnel to receive training so they would facilitate such difficult conversations. Like Carel, I believed this would enhance the quality of treatment. Like Carel, I thought phenomenological or interpretive research could yield the insights needed to construct appropriate educational scenarios. But reflecting on Carel's and Frank's books allowed me to see another possibility.

Just because you can't buy steak at Home Depot doesn't keep you from shopping elsewhere. If the medical establishment is neither prepared to nor capable of responding to illness, there is nothing preventing patients from looking elsewhere for support. The basic answer to the question, "Why am I not treated as a person by medical personnel," is simply this—they are not in a position to help one make meaning of suffering. Ironically, this may be the ultimate respect for the particularities of each person's unique confrontation with mortality. Medical personnel have no answers, no treatment, for existential questions. For them to pretend otherwise would be hubris.

It takes at least 12 years of post-secondary schooling to become a reasonably competent physician. It is likely that Carel spent as

---

7   Arthur Frank, p. 101.

much time becoming a competent philosopher. Is it realistic or reasonable to expect physicians (and other health care personnel) to become competent in both areas? Iconic images of competent AND caring doctors permeate the popular media, instilling an expectation that health care professionals should attend holistically to the person, not just the disease. In our fear and suffering, we mistake these fictionalized, ideal images for reality. Indeed some medical personnel come close, but it may be time to see them as the exception rather than the norm.

I have a friend who was diagnosed with pancreatic cancer which is typically fatal within a few months of diagnosis. Scans revealed a tumor entwined around a major blood vessel feeding the liver. Removing the tumor but leaving the liver reasonably intact would entail a very complex, not very common surgical procedure. If I faced my friend's situation, who would I want in the operating room—a highly skilled surgeon or caregiver who is responsive to my fear. Ideally, both would be nice. But if I have to choose, I would take the skilled surgeon.

Periodically the public safety agencies in my city hold disaster preparedness drills in which medical personnel must deal with overwhelming numbers of patients. At the pre-hospital level, emergency personnel triage the injured and the ill, sorting the dead from the living, the critically wounded from the salvageable. These are harsh terms, but they fit the harshness of the situation. With limited time and resources and far too many patients to treat, energy is expended on those who are most likely to survive and recover. As patients arrive at emergency departments another level of triage is performed, prioritizing patients in terms of severity and treatability of injuries. These simulations of extreme decision making bring into focus a dynamic that may operate more subtly on a day-to-day basis for medical personnel who deal with life-threatening conditions like heart attacks and cancer. There is a never-ending flow of patients into their examination rooms. How should they spend their time? Moving from one patient to the next to the next—offering the treatment(s) they know how to provide? Or do they linger with fewer patients offering emotional support during a prolonged existential struggle? Granted this may be a false dichotomy. If we had more physicians, if they were trained differently, if insurance paid for healing the soul as well as the body, then the dichotomy might disappear. With the allocation of sufficient resources, we could have both treatment and care. Yet, as the battle over health care reform rages on in the United States, we cannot even agree that all children should receive basic health care services. Lobbying for a public policy that supports caring as well as treatment seems quaintly quixotic.

What, then, might be done on an individual level? Given that it is more likely that Home Depot will begin to sell steak than the medical establishment will respond to existential suffering, I, for one, am turning my energies elsewhere. As Frank nears the end of his reflections on sinking through his illness to discover a new way of living, he argues quite persuasively and poignantly that those who become ill have a responsibility to:

> ...witness their own suffering and to express this experience so that the rest of us can learn from it. Of course others must be willing to learn; society's reciprocal responsibility is to see and hear what ill people express.[8]

Carel, like Frank, has chosen to accept this responsibility by writing about her experience of life-threatening illness. Those who read their words demonstrate a willingness to see, to hear, and to learn from their pain, fear, and struggle. Being present to the suffering of others respects and honors their life. Attending to their stories may help us traverse our own health crises with greater dignity and grace. Of course, none of this is certain. But as the horizon of my own death draws closer, this seems more practical than expecting the whole medical establishment to change.

---

8   Arthur Frank, p. 123.

8

Where Do We Turn for Comfort?

By the time I finished writing "Shopping for Steak at Home Depot," I decided to postpone tackling another thorny issue. Namely, if we abandon the expectation that health care personnel should respond supportively to the existential suffering precipitated by life-threatening disease, to whom should we turn for comfort? The following responses broke through the protective cocoon of procrastination and pushed me back to the keyboard. My son-in-law, an emergency medicine physician, said he did not disagree with the basic thesis of my essay, but raised the question:

> How many lay people are capable of giving such empathy and understanding to these patients, even without the added duty of treating the physical illness?

The second response from a friend who has devoted her professional life to addressing issues of health and wellness as well as medical ethics commented:

Your reflections raised some broader issues about
human nature, the nature of suffering, etc. If we can't
expect physicians to see us holistically, then where
do we go for support when we are ill...really ill? If
I were seriously ill, I'm not sure if anyone would
be interested in hearing about my deepest fears, my
experiential angst, my musings about how my sense
of self was undergoing a radical make over. This is
a load few people are able to bear (or have time to
pick up and carry). It also implies a profound sense
of intimacy, where the ill person "lets it all hang out"
and hopes that the details won't be crushing to the
listener. I wonder if this type of exchange happens
very often. Here's my thought. Like it or not, illness
is a lonely place each person navigates on his own.
Along the way, there are those who help, mostly
by listening, less by conversing. Still, it's a solitary
journey. Are better communication skills enough to
make a difference? I'm not sure!

My friend's response is particularly poignant since she had faced
breast cancer several years earlier.

Carel rails against friends and family who do and do not mention
her illness. At a dinner party she is reduced to tears and rage by an
insensitive guest who asks why she and her new husband are not
planning to have children. In another anecdote, she tells a friend that
she has lost nearly 50 per cent of her lung capacity in a short time.
The friend responds, "so if you lose another 50 percent next year..."
The sentence trails off as the friend realizes the implication of what
she is saying, but Carel says, "I never discussed my illness with her
again." Carel is equally resentful of two acquaintances who never
follow through on their promise to be in touch after they learn of her
illness. Eventually Carel admits:

...people are damned if they do and damned if they
don't. If they ask questions, I feel uncomfortable, as

if they are prying. If they say nothing, I think they are selfish, self-centered, oblivious to my plight. If it is difficult to talk about illness, it is especially hard for ill people. But what I learned from my illness is that in times of hardship, grief and loss, there is no need for original, illuminating phrases. There is nothing to say other than the most banal stuff: "I am sorry for your loss"; "This is so sad." Saying this—and listening—are the best ways to communicate with ill people. Or so I believe.[9]

Carel does allude to several individuals who apparently went beyond the banalities and offered substantive support. As a reader who feels guilty about my inadequate responses to both my sister's and mother's terminal illnesses, I wish Carel would have explained more fully what made the difference between supportive and non-supportive relationships. In this regard, I found Arthur Frank's exploration of the issue to be more nuanced and informative:

After persons receive a diagnosis of serious illness, the support they need varies as widely as humanity itself. Some want to have a family gathered around them, others need to be alone. Some need the assurance of immediate medical intervention, others have to have some time to decide what treatment they want. A physician may help one person by rushing in, another, by backing off. The caregiver's art is finding a way to allow the ill person to express his needs. Eventually a balance must be worked out between what the ill person needs and what the caregivers are able to provide. In order to find that balance, caregivers, whether professional, family, or friends, must help the ill person figure out what he

---

9   Havi Carel, *Illness: The Cry of the Flesh*. pp. 57-58.

> needs. Only then can they negotiate what they are
> prepared to provide.
>
> It takes time for an ill person to understand her
> needs. The caregiver cannot simply ask "What do
> you need?" and expect a coherent reply. A recently
> diagnosed person's life has already changed in more
> ways than she can grasp, and changes continue
> throughout critical illness. Part of what is "critical" is
> the persistence of change. Being critically ill means
> never being able to keep up with your own needs...[10]

Were I a friend of Carel's, I fear I would have had one all-or-nothing chance to get my response just right or be judged inadequate and banished. So I appreciate Frank's framing the issue as an on-going process involving the fluctuating needs and capacities of both the care-recipient and care-giver. It provides some solace as I look back on my mother's slow decline into oblivion. No matter what I did to provide for her care, I always felt I was playing catch-up. When I finally decided to move her from an independent living to a memory impairment facility, I realized the move had been long overdue. Two years later, the same realization came when, after months of agonizing, I finally moved her to a skilled nursing facility. I enrolled her in a hospice program thinking it would provide extra eyes to watch over her and extra hands to provide care. Only after several delays in her receiving treatment for eye infections did I realize the assisted living and the hospice staff were playing turf wars—each claiming the other should have been responsible for taking action. Always in hindsight I learned what care I should have been giving. Only in hindsight, well after she no longer communicated, did I let go of childish resentments that had built a firewall between

---

10   Arthur Frank, *At the Will of the Body.* p. 47.

my emotions and hers. Only after she was far beyond knowing me did I finally feel empathy rather than helpless despair for the existential fear that simmered just below her surface of fortitude and competence. Friends praise my dedication to my mother in her final years. In my heart, however, I know it was far too little and far too late. Like Carel, I am inclined to judge my inadequacies quite harshly. Frank's perspective engenders a modicum of forgiveness; my mother offered the best she was capable of during my childhood; I offered the best I was capable of during her dying. Neither was ideal, but we both muddled through to the best of our abilities.

This issue of unacknowledged, unacknowledgeable fear also played out in the four years of my sister's dying of kidney cancer. Here, too, Frank offers a source of reassurance. In exploring the "cost of appearances," Frank contends:

> The appearance most praised is "I'd hardly have known she was sick." At home the ill person must appear to be engaged in normal family routines; in the hospital she should appear to be just resting. When the ill person can no longer conceal the effects of illness, she is expected to convince others that being ill isn't that bad. The minimal acceptable behavior is praised faintly, as "stoical." But the ill person may not feel like acting good-humored and positive; much of the time it takes hard work to hold this appearance in place.[11]

Looking back, I can see times when Lilly gave me openings for discussing her thoughts and feelings about her death and dying. We watched a lot of feel-good television in her final months. Once, during *Touched by an Angel*, Lilly asked why I liked the show and

---

11   Arthur Frank. pp. 64-65.

whether I believed in angels. I responded with some innocuous remark that shut down the conversation. What might she have said had I turned the question around and asked her views on the subject of life after death? Every time she went for another test to see if a treatment had arrested the cancer's progress, I forced myself to call, dreading to hear her fear and despair when the news was bad. Yet, she would always seem to take the disappointment with equanimity. Did she really have that level of courage or was she making an effort to reassure and comfort me? As I lay alone crying in the middle of the night was she doing the same in her bedroom? As I steeled myself for the possibility that she would be worse at the dawn of each new day was she steeling herself to greet me with a cheerful hello? I will never know, because I couldn't bear to ask.

The closest we came was a conversation about John Edward, the psychic who claims he can speak with the dead. Lilly told me about his television show, *Crossing Over*, but I can no longer remember if we actually watched it together. However, Lilly did give me a secret password so I would know whether it was true if someone like John Edward claimed to be in contact with her. We joked about it, but again, I did not use it as an opportunity to discuss her views on death.

About a year after Lilly died, John Edward came to Pittsburgh on a book tour.[12] I figured I owed her a chance to communicate from the great beyond so I bought the book which included a ticket to a "reading." As I sat in the auditorium watching Edward work the crowd, my desire for him to "pick me" became stronger and stronger. How I longed to hear him say, "I'm getting something about [Lilly's secret word]." My hand could have shot up with certainty that my beloved sister still existed as herself in some dimension I do not yet understand. She might have let me know she was all right. She might have converted me from agnosticism to belief. I wanted desperately for some sign that would justify faith in angels and a hereafter. I tried to set aside my skepticism as Edward gave vague clues to which other audience members responded. Maybe if my mind were

---

12   John Edward, *After life: Answers from the other side,* 2003.

open, Lilly would have a better chance of coming through. Still, I couldn't help but notice how others answered Edward's general questions, providing him with the very information he was feeding back to them. Lilly, like me, had been a skeptic. How wise of her to provide a specific identifier that no one but me could possibly know. How surprised I was that I would gladly have responded to Edward had he said anything that remotely came close to her code word. At the end of the hour, I trailed out of the theater with no more certainty than when I had entered.

I must acknowledge that I have never been comfortable talking about my deepest emotions with family members. Perhaps my reluctance to broach the topics of fear and suffering is mine alone. Yet, both Carel and Frank contend there are endemic social constraints against such conversations. While this may be true for society at large, I congratulate myself on having a circle of close friends with whom I have had many serious conversations about a range of difficulties in my life and theirs. Then, a few months ago as I was talking about facilitating a series of discussions on adult sibling loss, one friend said, "I have had many questions I wanted to ask you, but I was afraid to bring them up." I was surprised. She had been one of my confidantes as I struggled with sorrow over the illnesses and deaths of my sister and mother. Surely I had let her know I was willing to talk about these painful subjects. Then I realized that I had avoided discussing the death of her infant daughter. I, too, had many questions, but was afraid to ask. It was not (I think) a fear of my being overwhelmed with sadness for her loss, but fear of reactivating the rawness of her grief.

Carel says it is especially difficult for the person who is ill to raise the subject of her illness. This challenges my long-held assumption that I should follow the ill person's lead. If they want to talk, I would respond. If they did not raise the subject, I would respect their privacy. Yet, the experiences with my sister and now with my friend suggest that I was deluding myself. Frank contends it is unrealistic to expect someone reeling from a diagnosis of life-threatening illness to have a clear-cut answer to the question, "What do you need?" It is just as unrealistic for me to think a person would state explicitly, "If you don't mind, I'd like to discuss how I feel about dying." The invitations for such conversations are likely to be far more subtle, far more oblique. The likelihood of missing (or ignoring) the cues is high—not out of callous indifference, but out of mutual consideration and protection. As my friend suggested, sharing one's deepest existential angst is an act of incredible intimacy. Perhaps that is why we invest so much longing for health care professionals to deal with the issue of existential suffering. We already suspend socially inscribed boundaries for personal intimacy to permit diagnosis and treatment of disease. Perhaps it is logical to extend the clinician's right of access to the most intimate recesses of our psyches in order to offer care for life-altering illness. Still, I have concluded this is unfair to those schooled in the science of treating disease. So where do I turn?

Were I a religious person, I might consider clergy a reasonable alternative. Indeed, I have met many individuals whose faith brings great solace. Without wishing to offend anyone, I must confess that for me this would be false comfort. Carel turned to philosophy to wrestle with her existential fears. Drawing from the works of Heidegger and Epicurus, she constructs a reasoned case for not fearing death. That, too, feels like false comfort. By far, I resonate most strongly with Frank's conclusion that sharing our stories of illness and existential angst can bring comfort both to the teller and to the listener. These stories do not necessarily make such conversations any less awkward, but they open spaces for exploration. For many, the exploration leads into unfamiliar and scary terrain. We are likely to stumble, to feel lost, to be anxious. Yet acknowledging our uncertainties and trusting our compassion may allow us to give and receive support in unexpected ways. Ultimately, none of us— even the most skilled health care professionals—can stop another's trajectory toward death. But through our caring, even when less than perfect, we may help to alleviate the loneliness of the journey.

PART 2

INTRODUCTION

Stories of Sibling Loss

In the winter and spring of 1999, I began to interview men and women who had survived the death of an adult brother or sister. One of the women I interviewed was the pastor at an elegant stone church located in a small village north of Pittsburgh. As we walked from her office into the library where we would hold our conversation, she mentioned that Tiffany had made the church's windows and that they were in the process of being cleaned. Curious, we detoured into the sanctuary flooded by light filtered through magnificent stained glass renderings of the Stations of the Cross. "The windows are made of layers of glass," Janet explained. "Dirt gets between the layers and dulls the light. So they have to be taken apart and cleaned." I made the appropriate "oohs" and "aahs" of appreciation, but I couldn't really visualize what this cleaning process entailed. I had imagined men on scaffolds, buffing the delicate glass with soft cloths. Clearly this wasn't the case. "They remove the windows," Janet continued, "and take them to their workshop in the West End. That's where they do the cleaning."

In the weeks following the interview, I continued to puzzle over the process of cleaning the stained glass windows. Eventually, I asked for and received permission to visit the workshop. There, on the second floor of a dimly lit, drafty, old wooden building, lay hundreds of pieces of glass. No two were exactly the same—some were large, others small; some were delicate, milky pastel; others were deep, clear blue or green or red. "First we trace a template of the window," my guide explained. "We number all of the pieces as we take the window apart. Then we clean each individual piece." I noticed a cluster of pale pink and peach colored glass. "Tiffany would use layers of glass to create the exact color effect he wanted. The ones you're looking at are part of Jesus' face. When the sun comes through the window, the glass takes on the color of skin tones." Suddenly I got it and was stunned. Effects that painters create on canvas with oils or watercolors, Tiffany created with glass and sunlight. Each detail, each straight line, each curve of a hand or swirl of cloth was created with glass chosen for clarity, color, texture, and the way it would catch the light, not in isolation, but in combination with other pieces.

This layering of glass to create a picture offers a metaphor for the compilation of stories that follows. Each story provides a brief portrait of sibling relationships clouded by the shadow of death. In all, I conducted thirteen conversational interviews. As might be expected, each conversation evolved in a unique way, guided by the thoughts and feelings that arose in my interviewee, in me and between the two of us. Often we digressed as one or the other of us shared ideas that were triggered in the course of the conversation. In general, however, the conversations were guided by a fourfold intent to gain glimpses into:

- the personality and life of the person who died;
- the relationship between the deceased and surviving brother or sister;
- how the sibling's death had affected the survivor; and
- how the surviving sibling dealt with their grief.

The individuals I interviewed were randomly selected only in the sense that I happened to know them, someone referred them, or they contacted me in response to an announcement I had posted. The resulting group is, admittedly, small and homogeneous. All my conversational partners and I were white, middle-class, native-born U.S. citizens. Our experiences are embedded in and shaped by this cultural milieu. A friend from Kenya whose brother died from cancer confirms that her experience of grief has been shaped by other cultural norms. So I offer the following narratives, not as a scientific study of grief, but as heartfelt expressions from those who were kind enough to share their story with me.

As I pondered the conversations we had shared, I was struck by the ordinariness of the lives that had been lost. "Ordinary" may sound pejorative, as though the sibling who died wasn't important, but that is not what I mean. The siblings I heard about had lived and died within a circle of family and friends. Their lives did not play out in wide public arenas. They were not celebrities. They may never have had even 15 minutes of fame. They were not heroic in some grand scheme of things. They did not die in the service of some cause or their country. Whatever contributions they made were within the scope of work, family, and community. Yet, their deaths deeply touched their surviving siblings. I was also struck by how unassuming my interviewees were. Several said, "Well, I'm not sure I have anything important to say, but if it will help you or somebody else, I'm happy to talk with you." What came through was a sense of each person's quiet decency, dignity, and caring.

Indeed, the stories that were shared did help me as I grieved the anticipated and final loss of my sister. By passing them along, I hope that they may help others as well. In using the metaphor of layered glass, I want to make clear that my aim is not to present broad, scientific generalizations about grief and grieving. Rather, it is to honor the unique circumstances of each individual's experience. I recognize that readers may resonate more deeply with some of the stories than others. To facilitate the process of locating stories of greatest potential interest, I have loosely grouped them, first by the circumstances of death and second by the type of sibling relationship (i.e., sister-sister, sister-brother, brother-brother).

For Alana, Terry, Tina, and Marion death intruded unexpectedly. Their grieving took place after a sudden, unanticipated loss. All four were close to the sibling who passed away—Alana, Terry, and Tina to their sisters; Marion to her brother. Of all the stories I heard, Alana's stands out because of the tragic circumstances that accidentally claimed her sister's life.

For May, Janet, Rachel, Marta, and Ned there was a realization that death could be imminent, either because their sibling suffered from a longstanding health problem (May, Marta) or was diagnosed with a terminal illness (Janet, Rachel, Ned). While the valence of grief might differ from an expectable rather than sudden death, the finality of death still came as a shock and precipitated a grieving process. May's story is unique among those I gathered in that she is one of 13 siblings. While a number of surviving siblings had had very close bonds with the sister or brother who died, Marta had been estranged from her sister for a number of years when her sister passed away. Janet's story stands out because of her sister's decline through dementia. As I mentioned in the Prologue to the book, Rachel's loss was the most distant, her brother having died 30 years before we talked.

Three individuals had experienced the loss of two siblings. In Ronald's case he had had virtually no relationship with a severely disabled brother and had been very close to a sister who died unexpectedly, even though she had had serious health issues. Kendra and Kate each lost a brother in an accident. Years later, Kendra lost a sister to cancer and Kate lost another brother due to a medical mistake.

I have also included Delilah's story although at the time of our conversation, her sister was in remission from cancer. As a close friend, Delilah served as a sounding board for me as I struggled to sort through feelings and thoughts about my own experience with my sister and those arising from the interviews. Delilah's sister subsequently died after a prolonged decline from dementia.

The stories that follow are my narrative distillations of the interview transcripts. In crafting these stories, I have tried to stay true to the spirit and words of the conversations. At the same time, I have tried to eliminate the repetitions that inevitably occur in free flowing conversations and to highlight points that I felt offered a different perspective or experience. Again, my aim has been to portray the variations among my interviewees' experiences so they might offer layered insights into the grief of sibling loss.

9

ALANA and ELLIE

Alana is one of four siblings—two brothers and a younger sister Ellie who died in 1999 at age 33. Alana was 38 when Ellie died and 41 at the time of my interview with her. When I asked Alana about the circumstances of Ellie's death, she responded, "It's a complicated story." Indeed, the events in the aftermath of Ellie's death were complicated. But the details of a young woman's untimely death are simply, starkly, tragic.

Ellie was a studious, sensible child who loved to read. She went to college and earned a Master's degree in clinical psychology. She worked at a New England college where she tutored students, including all the athletes, who had problems with education. It was a fabulous job that Ellie reluctantly left when her fiancé took a job in Charlotte. Although Ellie didn't particularly like Charlotte, she found another college advising position. Ellie's fiancé, Wade, had rented a 3-story town house for them, one in a cluster of four attached units. She had been there about three months when our mother went to visit. As they toured the house, Ellie showed our mother the attic. There were no fire walls, and they could peer into the neighbors' units and actually see their belongings. Shortly after moving in, Ellie and Wade wrote a carefully documented letter to the builder, detailing how hazardous the "shared attic" could be.

On Tuesday of the week Ellie died she had to give a presentation 50 miles from Charlotte. Her Honda's air conditioning was shot, so Wade offered, "Take the new Lexus. I'll use yours." That evening, as he pulled into the garage, a friend called. Concentrating on his conversation, he left the car and entered the house. When Ellie arrived home, she parked the Lexus outside and joined Wade. About 9:00 that evening, she was talking to our mom on the phone and complained about an unbearable headache and nausea.

The first inkling of trouble came on Wednesday morning when Wade did not show up for work. Ellie's colleagues also thought it was odd that she did not call to say she was taking the day off. Still, no one was concerned enough to check in with them. On Thursday morning, a neighbor thought it was strange that the Lexus was still in the same position and that newspapers were piling up. What really caught her attention, however, was the water trickling out of the garage. Feeling something was not right, the neighbor called 911 at about 7:30 in the morning. The Fire Department and police came. They started tearing down the doors, one by one, and finding the bodies.

Investigations by the police and FBI pieced together what happened. Wade, distracted by his phone call and forgetting that the Honda's ignition had to be manually turned off, left the car running in the closed garage. It was still running two days later and was so hot it had triggered the sprinkler system, which led to the trickle of water and the neighbor's alerting the authorities. Carbon monoxide from the car went into the sprinkler system which, along with the air conditioning, shot the gas all the way up to the attic, where it spread to the connected units. Luckily, the neighbors directly next to Ellie and Wade were away on vacation. Two other neighbors died. In the farthest unit, a man and his son had collapsed; the son suffered brain damage.

The authorities determined that Ellie, Wade and the others had died sometime between Tuesday night and Wednesday morning. It was such a senseless death. We kept going over and over it. How could it have happened? The video cameras at Wade's bank showed him getting into the Honda. After her presentation, Ellie said good bye to all her colleagues, and they were commenting, "Oh, you have the Lexus today." Then later there was the phone call to our mother. It was just so bizarre. Ellie and Wade were getting married in three months. Their friends had just received a newsletter spelling out the details of their wedding. Then they learned of their deaths. It was all over the news; it was on CNN.

The police first reported that the incident was caused by the Honda that Ellie drove. We got frustrated, because who cares about those details? They're gone. Wade's family turned on us, saying, "What was your sister thinking?" Then it came out that all of her books and things were in the Lexus. That was so irrelevant. There was nothing we could do but move on.

We were all still in shock. In terms of specifics—who, what, when and where—we didn't care. I had just lost my little sister, so the details didn't matter. Afterward, there were huge lawsuits. The investigators determined it was an accident. We had to deal with that; tell people, "My God, no, it was not suicide." It was just a twist of fate. Like when I heard about 9/11. One man decided to fly home early to be with his family so he booked a new flight and died. I worked with people who were always on the Web checking out the chain of events and whispering among themselves. Aside from having a loss, I was having to deal with ignorance. That really upset me.

The weekend before Ellie died, she flew in for a visit; to have a sisterly weekend prior to taking the big plunge. We just sat in bed and drank coffee and had good girl talk. It's funny. I did something I never do. I called my mom and said, "Why don't you spend the weekend with us?" My sister and I rarely had quality time together. We were always on the phone and emailed, but in-person time was harder to fit in. Yet, I felt compelled to invite my mother. She stayed with us Friday and Saturday night and went with me when I took Ellie to the airport. That was another twist of things. If I can look at it in terms of the positives instead of looking at the 'why's' I would say we were given a wonderful weekend. It still feels like it was yesterday.

Ellie and Wade were both dedicated Catholics. Ellie had even postponed the start of her career to travel to Micronesia and Belize as a Jesuit volunteer. I used say, "Ellie, either you're going to be the next president or some kind of spiritual leader." Ellie had so much to offer. They did a dedication in Micronesia—all her little students— and everywhere she had been in Belize, and the colleges where she did her undergraduate and graduate work. I don't ask, "Why did she have to go?" Instead I'll think, "She was such a beautiful person inside and out. She could have touched so many more lives." Then I'll say to myself, "She's still touching lives, and she's still doing her work."

I'm fortunate to have a very supportive group of friends, but I didn't want anyone around me. I chose to shut them out. I look at my own family and how we deal with loss. There are so many variations. I have to respect everyone's individuality, and that's very hard. My mother is so strong. She has her good days and her bad days. I have two brothers, and I love them dearly, but it's not quite the same as with my sister. One brother can't talk about it; won't talk about it. Actually both brothers are very much like that. I talk about her lovingly, like she's still part of my life. I just want to talk about her and cry quietly with music on and a nice bottle of wine. One brother finds this absurd, like are you drinking or what? But it's how I choose to live my life right now."

I wasn't married when Ellie died. When I first met my husband, Ryan, he asked, "How many brothers and sisters do you have?" I was not prepared for this question. It just took me by the throat. I didn't know how to answer. I didn't know if I should say, "There are four of us. Well, there are three. Well, there were four, now there are three." All these variations went through my head within seconds. Do I deny my sister? Yet, I can't burden him with that.

Before meeting me, Ryan had asked a couple of guys, "Hey, who's this Alana?" They said, "You know what, it's a long story. You don't want to go there. She's got some issues." So that's how I was viewed. Because I went around bawling, I could see where they might say something like that. I have since approached one fellow, and he admitted, "Yeah, I did say that. But I didn't know what to say to him." These are well educated people. You would think they would know better.

So Ryan heard, "she has issues." Nevertheless he approached me. Small talk, small talk. Then he asked that question, and I didn't know how to answer. I just started to cry, and said, "You're going to have to excuse me." We were in a public place. He turned to my girlfriends and asked, "What did I say?"

They said, "Oh…"

Ryan's a very gentle, caring, understanding man who didn't want the specifics of how she died. He simply said if I ever needed a person to talk to, he was there. That was just the greatest thing. Ellie was the most compassionate of all of us, the most soothing. That's how Ryan is. So with Ellie gone, Ryan has stepped up to the plate. It's amazing to have someone like that in my life now, to fill that void.

I learned through all this that people don't know how to handle things. I have a lot of friends who would say, "Here comes Alana. Don't talk about it. Everyone be nice. Everyone, shhhh." Then, one of their fathers was ill or dying, and I said, "Hey, are you trying to protect me. I'm 40 years old. I don't need to be protected." Talking about death is healthy. Society can accept the loss of a parent or a grandparent. But when you say, "I lost a sister," it's like, "Oooh I don't want to go there." They would rather hear about a football game. They can deal with stuff like that, but talk about the death of a sibling and my heart bleeds. I was yearning to talk to people but I knew they didn't want to hear it. The sister of my oldest and closest friend died of cancer. We have a mutual male friend who said to me, "You know, Alana, I couldn't deal with her anymore. It was all my sister, blah, blah, blah. We'd go out to have a glass of wine, it was woe, woe, woe." So he shunned her. People don't know how to deal with it, until it happens to them. Then they'll know. Guaranteed if his brother or sister died he would call me immediately saying. "Oh, my God, what do I?" It's taken me a long time to understand that it's out of ignorance; they don't know what to say. People would say, "I can only imagine what you are going through." No you don't. You don't have any idea. So don't even pretend that you can understand. Just say, "Hey, let's go for a cup of coffee or glass of wine sometime. Maybe we can talk about your sister."

So, if someone has passed away, my approach is not to say, "I'm sorry." The word "sorry" is just like "good morning," "how are you." It's robbed of meaning. It's not heartfelt. Now I'll say, "tell me about your sister; tell me about your brother. What do you miss about your brother or sister? What's the most wonderful thing she or he did?" I find that their face brightens. They'll say something like, "My sister's a big joker." Something of that sort to bring back a fond memory. If I don't know the person, I will say, "I'm sorry to hear about your sister's death," but I say it heartfelt.

My friend whose sister died from cancer had time to consciously be aware of the inevitable. She was able to be by her sister's bedside and share things with her. I was robbed of that. However, Ellie and I talked so frequently that I was able to do those things while Ellie was alive as opposed to while she was dying. I always try to tell my friends who haven't spoken to their siblings or their parents, "Don't wait till it's too late and you are at their bedside saying, 'I love you.' Don't wait." People complain, "You have no idea how bad he or she was, or mean or this or that or whatever." I feel sorry for the person who has closed the door on a sibling based on some stupid misunderstanding. What they are mourning may be a lot of guilt. Thank God, I don't have that. The day I took her to the airport, I held her and said I loved her. Not a time went by that she didn't know that. So instead of having to say "I love you" when she's six feet under, I was telling her while she was alive. Prior to Ellie's death, my brothers didn't really say "love you" to one another. Now it's "hey I love you." Our differences don't last. We try to nip disagreements right away. "Listen. Let me tell you why I'm upset right now." We never did that before. The day you realize there's nothing you can do, you start looking at your own life and say, "Maybe someone is looking out above me. I'd better be a good person. Someone's watching."

Ellie knew I loved her every day. I think I was pretty good sister. Sure there are things I should or could have said. Maybe listened more. But for the most part I was there when she needed me. Now, don't get me wrong. We fought a lot, too. I wouldn't want to change that either, because that was healthy. She'd express her opinion and me mine. That's part of the program. We can do the same for mourning. I light candles all the time. That's my little tribute. I like the solace of lighting candles. I lie down and think about her. My aunt called me on Ellie's birthday. I told her, "I just don't want to forget Ellie. I don't want to forget those details that I miss." I want them to be part of my life. I've planted my sister's favorite flowers around my house.

I have pictures of Ellie throughout the house. I've talked to other people who can't have pictures up. I miss my sister's face. I miss holding her hands. Just her gentleness. I miss that bond. I miss the advice she'd give me. Sometimes friends give advice that might benefit them just a tad. When Ellie gave me advice she wasn't intimidated to tell me things, even if I didn't want to hear them. She could tell me something, and I wouldn't want to attack her, because I knew that it came from the heart. She had only my well-being in mind. I miss that.

Ellie was always the solid one. I had jumped into an earlier marriage, just jumped into things. Education was secondary for me. I just had fun with dating and what not. Nothing illegal. One day I said, "You know, Ellie, I admire you. Going on with your education, your masters, and then some. Your professors have to give their approval; you have to speak another language as well as maintain a 3.5. Then teaching all over the country. You are my mentor."

Ellie looked at me and said, "You've got to be kidding, right? Why do you think I had to get into education? I wasn't any good in sports. Look at what I had to live up to. Everyone always talked about Alana and her beauty. I said 'Okay, I can't do that. So I'll be in my books. I'll be as educated and smart as I can'."

I just looked at her and said, "You've got to be kidding me." We probably made that revelation about three years prior to her death. Can you imagine how someone could view me as someone to live up to? Here I am looking up at her. We were very, very different. She was quiet, didn't talk to people much. She wasn't as outgoing. Whereas me; I talk to anybody and everybody. It wasn't until two years prior to her death that I accepted her for who she was. She would read a book instead of talking to me. I would watch TV; she would read a book. She hit it on the head when she told me to accept people for who they are and what they like to do and not expect them to do what I do. I miss her advice; I wish I had listened more.

We grew up in a Catholic family and always went to church on Sunday, but that doesn't necessarily mean we were very religious. We just sat in the pews, said the regular everyday prayers, prior to dinner and stuff. Ellie was the one who had the strong religious belief, who had the most faith. She'd always put a religious spin on things, while I was like, "Whatever." I was somewhat the rebel. My faith was there, but I was never really a strong believer. Then after Ellie's death, it took a big spin. I was like, "Okay, why her?" At the time I was single. My marriage had gone sour; I had gone through a divorce. I was dating this guy and that guy. My sister had so much to give. I couldn't understand why God had to take the cream of the crop so to speak. A priest who's a good friend of the family— who not only prepared Ellie's eulogy, but also did my daughter's baptism—shared an analogy with me that really, truly, makes more sense than anything else. Ellie's cup was full. It was her time to be called. Was it coincidental that she took that car? Who knows? It wasn't until Ellie died that my religious beliefs became stronger. I firmly believe that Ellie is in a better place now. My biggest loss is that I miss her. Selfishly. I want her here. I want to share my life with her. I miss that. I tell myself she is in a far better place; she's doing her job somewhere up there.

After Ellie's death, meeting a man was the last thing I wanted. I had been through a marriage. I felt, "That's it, I'm done. I'm not meant to have any children." Pittsburgh's a small town. Everyone's kind of dating someone already. Everyone knows everyone. You've got to dot your I's and cross your T's. You do one bad thing and you're pegged. So when I met Ryan, I felt it was like a second chance; it was a gift. Then to have Ava. There's not a day that goes by that I don't thank God. I say, "My daughter has a guardian angel."

The other day, I picked up the portable phone and was walking and talking to my mother. In a matter of 30 seconds, I was like,

"Where's Ava? Where did she go?" She was sitting in the bathtub. Fortunately there wasn't any water in the tub, but I was hysterical She will see her sponge and toys in the tub, but she can't reach them. You have to lean over the silver rail of the sliding doors. How did she manage to get over that? Why hadn't she fallen in head first; why hadn't she cried? How did she get in and spin around? I thought, "Could it possibly have been Ellie?" It's like Ava was just lifted up and set down. She was sitting there with this really bewildered look. So I say we have a guardian angel looking out after all of us. It's little things like that that I try to view positively. Instead of physically seeing Ellie, I know that she's here in our presence. I'll wish Ellie could see Ava. Then I say, "Wait a minute. She CAN see her. She sees her 24/7."

I still speak with her. I ran over the vacuum cord the other day and damaged it. I said, "Oh, Ellie!" Just little things like that. It's beneficial, because I don't want to forget her. I want to be able to share who she was with my daughter. A year or two goes by, three, four, five; you don't ever forget but it's not as immediate. The anniversary of her death and her birthday are still very special days I kind of dedicate to her memory. I go to church, light a candle, so we don't forget.

We were advised to get some counseling; maybe get some medication like Prozac or Zoloft to get through the hump. I thought, "What if I go on some drug and am balanced? Then a year later I go off it, and I'm a wipe out." I decided I'd better just deal with it now. Just do what I want. Cry when I want.

Trust me. I did lose a lot of my faith after Ellie died, asking "Why?" With cancer you can say "that's why." You can ask, "Why did she have to get it?" We don't know, but there is something scientific to back that up. A person who has a disease can get their anger out, maybe daily. When people die in car accidents, murder, things like that, it's a different kind of death; a different kind of mourning. My sister's death was horrific. You are mad at the world. I think that was a natural phase that one has to go through. I read so many books on dealing with grief. I'd throw them on the floor.

Malarkey! Don't give me a scientific view on why and what I should be doing next.

A psychologist friend of mine gave me a book that looked at the literature on death and dying. It said we make seven assumptions about it; that we go through stages of grief in this way. Then the author asked, "Is there any evidence to support that this is how we do it?" She looked systematically at all the research and found no evidence to support our assumption about the way we are supposed to grieve. She looked at the idea that after you've mourned, you are done mourning, like you wouldn't think about the person who is gone. That's so absurd. Why would anybody who's been alive and lost anybody, ever dream that suddenly you would stop thinking about that person. Our society doesn't really have good ideas about how to deal with death. You have to customize it to who you are and what the relationship was between you and the person you lost. There isn't a book out there that can say what you should do.

The day you come to terms with what has happened and not ask "why" but "how" is the day you'll come to peace with yourself. That revelation did not hit me right away. I was mad at the world for a while, but there was nothing I could do to bring her back. Instead I just think about fond memories, about happy things. What made her laugh? I remember watching Kathy Lee and Regis. Ellie said, "I hate that woman. She gets on my nerves. She's loud and obnoxious." I said, "I kind of like her. In a strange way, I feel sorry for her. She had a bad rap." Ellie said, "You kind of remind me of her at times." I said, "Shut the hell up. What do you mean? You just said she's obnoxious." She said, "Well, you know…" I laughed because I saw Kathy Lee on TV and thought, "My God, she is a bit obnoxious." I'll say, "Hi, Ellie. You had one on me." I live through memories of her. After a while, I realized, "What can I learn through her death and do what she would do and how she would touch people's lives." Through her death, I changed; I settled my butt down; I matured.

The biggest thing my sister's death taught me is not to be afraid of death. That was huge. I can tell you honestly there is nothing that I have not yet done that I wish I would do. In the two and a half years that my sister has been dead, I have done so many things and traveled so many places. I told Ryan, "If I should die tomorrow don't cry for me. Promise you won't mourn for me. I want you to move on with your life, to find another woman. I want that woman to be good, so that she can raise our daughter." He said, "Oh, my God, what are you saying." I said, "No. No. There you go. You're doing what everybody else does. You don't want to talk about it." Let's face it; it could happen. I said goodbye to my sister on Sunday and she died Tuesday. You never know. This might sound a bit morbid, but I have lived a good life. Even at 40 years of age. Yes, I would love to see Ava grow up. I would love to grow old with my husband. But every day I've had some happiness so I'm not scared of death anymore. I say that with all my heart, because I haven't been married all that long. I haven't had my daughter all that long. At least I've experienced what it was like to have a wonderful husband and a wonderful daughter.

Also, I see things differently now. My mom and I were in Sarasota and saw the ocean. Isn't it amazing how the shells come up. Look at that blue sky. So what if it's raining; we need it so we can have flowers. All these things were always there. But I took all that for granted. So when I tell my husband that death doesn't scare me because I've lived a good life, I mean it.

For a good six months I hated the world. If during that time you told me that I would be talking like this, I would have said, "Oh, please." I was telling a friend, "You have to look at the kind of person you are." You have to know that when something tragic happens, how did you handle it; what kind of person are you. Are you one to have to hit the bottle, to shut the door to people, to pull people in? That's the same way you're going to be when you lose a sibling. At a different level, but you have to know yourself, how you handle adversities.

When Ava was born, she was breach. Early in the pregnancy they told me she was going to be diagnosed with Trisemony 18. I had to deal with my pregnancy not knowing what the hell was going to go wrong, what I'd have to deal with. My husband who is very gentle and kind said, "Alana, we can deal with this together, right?" I said, "Yeah." When she was born she was perfect. Not to say that if she were born any differently that she wouldn't still be special.

The biggest thing for me is to truly understand what kind of person you are and how you accept and handle things. There isn't a book out there that says what you should and shouldn't do. It's okay if you want to kick people out. It's okay if you want people around. It's okay if all I want to do is listen to music. If you're not going through step one, don't think, "Oh my God, what's wrong with me." One book said there are four different ways to grieve and it described the sequence of how it should be. Well, you know the fourth one could be the first one; the first one may never happen. Tailor your own mourning process—just like when you tailor a diet to what you like and have to have. About 20 years ago, my grandmother said to me, "Usually give things about 3 months or so. You'll see things differently and maybe then your 'why's' will make sense." So I knew that I was going to feel like shit for three months or more. I had to just bear it. Three months could be a long time, too long, but at least I knew it would come to an end. In a death situation, know that it's going to be as long as you need it to be or make it to be. The day you accept that it happened, the day that you know that you can't do anything, it's going to shorten everything. There isn't a day that goes by that I don't think of Ellie, don't miss her. It's okay to mourn my sister for the rest of my life. I can do it privately. My husband doesn't even know half the time what I think or what I do during the day. Ava will be asleep in my arms at nap time and tears fall on her and I'll say, "Oh, Ellie, she's so perfect and so beautiful." It's okay.

10

TERRY and MELANIE

Sisters Terry and Melanie were the only two children in their family. Melanie died of heart failure in 1998 at the age of 30 when Terry was 32. I interviewed Terry four years after her sister's death.

Although Melanie was quiet and wasn't in with the popular crowd, everyone knew who she was. She had been in the high school band and was home-coming queen. Melanie was a don't-throw-your-litter-out kind of person. She was vegetarian for a while. She was the cleanest hippie I've ever known, because it would take her two hours to get that natural look.

Melanie and the boy she had been dating for over eight years were Dead Heads. After graduating from high school, whenever Melanie had a vacation, they would go to Grateful Dead concerts. During this phase, she took those over-the-counter mini-thins or two-way tablets that you can get at any grocery store, any roadside gas station. They have ephedrine in them and truck drivers use them to keep awake. She would take those, because they were traveling from state to state, trying to get in as many concerts as they could in a weekend. She took those to the point of abuse, like 20 a day.

When she and her boyfriend broke up, she got rid of all her memorabilia—her Grateful Dead things, her pictures, everything. It was really traumatic for her. She got rid of all the pills since she didn't need them anymore. She was naturally skinny. People would always go, "Oh, she's dieting." She was bulimic at one time when she was young. Then she got herself out of that. But she never had a good self-image. She was beautiful, but she thought, "Oh, I'm so ugly. I'm fat." Our mom was really abusive when we were little. She had been sexually abused when she was young, so it carried over. I don't agree with some of Mom's ways of disciplining us, but I understand why she did it. Maybe that's where Melanie got some of her problems. Not feeling good enough.

After Melanie broke up with her boyfriend, she married a real loser on the rebound. He was abusive—verbally, mentally, physically. After she and her husband had a baby, she went back to work. They needed money. She had to do everything. Her husband wouldn't do diddly squat. He wouldn't even watch the baby while she went to the store for a gallon of milk. So she started taking ephedrine tablets. She also drank a lot of coffee. You're not supposed to take caffeine with ephedrine. She would get up at 4:30 in the morning to get herself ready. Then she'd get the baby up; cook him breakfast; make his lunch; bring him here; go to work. At the end of the day, she'd come here; pick him up; go home; clean; do everything. If the baby got up in the middle of the night, she had to be up. She was a really good mom.

I had married at 19 and moved to the South. I was always worried about Melanie. We grew up very close. She was always like my baby; I had to protect her. When my husband was offered a good job back in Pittsburgh, I was relieved to move back. "Whew," I thought. "I don't have to worry about her anymore. I can protect her." As it turned out, I had a year with Melanie before my worst fear happened. Out of nowhere. In the blink of an eye. I'm talking to her one minute; the next she's gone. You think you can protect someone, but you can't.

I had been talking on the phone with Melanie, but she had to hang up. She had just come home from work and was looking for her husband and child. When I called back to see if she had found them, there was no answer. I thought, "Maybe she's on the commode or something." I called back again, but still no answer. About five minutes later, her husband called, just screaming. He had walked into the house and Melanie was sitting on the couch; she was blue. He was in hysterics. He couldn't even call the ambulance. Couldn't even think. He said, "I'm just going to throw her in the car and get her to the hospital." I said, "Don't. Just stay." We got there before the ambulance did. She had wet herself. She had a very faint heart beat. My husband tried to do CPR; she started to throw up in his mouth. When the ambulance came, there wasn't anything they could do.

The emergency room doctor said she had a cardiovascular arrhythmia; an electrode in her heart automatically stopped. They have on her death certificate, accidental overdose of ephedrine, because they found so much in her system. I had asked the coroner, "Can you call me with the report?" He said, "I'm sorry. Her husband will have to give the okay." Well, you don't understand. She's been my sister for 30 years. She's been married to him for a year. Where does that give him all these rights? She's my family. She's my blood. It's not fair that siblings have no rights. The deputy coroner was very nice. I said, "Do me a favor. Her husband's stupid and he probably doesn't give a crap whether I know or not. Can you say, "Is it okay if I call your sister-in-law?" He did call me and let me know what they had found.

About two weeks before she died, she had started taking ephedrine, but she hadn't taken a lot, maybe five a day. I had the bottle and counted them. I did some research. I talked with the doctor two weeks later and asked, "Do you think she overdosed?" He said, "No. She would have had to take massive doses, and we would have found it in her stomach. She couldn't have taken that many pills." He thought it might be that her body wasn't cleaning them out of her system and they were building up. I called the deputy coroner to ask, "Do you take into consideration what they give her at the hospital or in the ambulance?" He said, "No we don't." So I said, "In all actuality, the high levels of ephedrine could have been because they were pumping it in trying to get her heart to start again." He said, "Yeah, that could be."

They did not find any illegal drugs in her body. They found Tylenol and ephedrine. That's it. She did not do illegal drugs. She was not a drinker. But the rumor mill got started and because her husband was a big pill popper, people would say, "Oh, we heard she was snorting cocaine," or "we heard she was trying to diet and starve herself," or "we heard she was on drugs and OD'd." It ticks me off that people are judging her when they don't know what happened. Nobody except the coroner, the doctor and the family know. I wish the coroner could change her death certificate, but he can't. It's not fair. But people who knew Melanie know better. I guess that's all that matters.

Because we got to her house before the ambulance, I could not get the picture of her lying there out of my head. I saw her on the gurney when they were taking her out to the ambulance. She had this stare. I know she looked at me. I kept yelling, "Just make it. You're going to make it. You're going to make it. You'll be okay." I kept yelling, "I love you. I love you." I hope she knows that. That's hard. Do they know?

I'm still really mad at the hospital about the way they handled her death. Her doctor was wonderful; I can't blame him. He tried his best. The hospital has only one doctor for the whole emergency room. You're in the waiting room with everybody else. There's a little room. They pull you into it and say, "Why don't you sit in here." All nicey-nice. The nurse said, "The doctor's going to be in." I just knew, but then she did one of those, "Don't worry. It's okay." He comes in and starts asking questions. "Are there heart conditions in your family? Did she have a history of blah, blah, blah?" All of a sudden he said, "I'm sorry. There's nothing we could do. We lost her." Right there in the emergency room where other people are right next to you.

She died at 12:30. At 2:00 they were taking her to St. Francis for the autopsy. That's not a lot of time. Don't leave her lying there with stuff in her. Clean her up. Let us come in. Let me hold her hand. Let me get a lock of hair or something. But they didn't do anything.

They almost didn't get her to the funeral home in time for the viewing. The coroner got called out on an emergency, so he couldn't do the autopsy till the next morning. It was crazy. It's like, now you're going to let her sit there, too? Does she not mean anything to anybody? You're just going to let her sit there overnight, till you can get to her. They had an hour to do the autopsy. Four people worked on her. Boom. That was it. It was hard walking into the funeral home and seeing her. It would probably have been hard seeing her at the hospital, but maybe her spirit was still with her; maybe she would have known we were there.

I'm also mad at the Herbalife places. GNC claims the FDA says ephedrine taken in certain doses is safe. When I called the FDA and told them about GNC's claim, they said, "We didn't say that." When I reported that Melanie's death could have been linked to ephedrine, the FDA said they wanted to pass legislation to limit the dose to 8mg per tablet not to exceed 24mg per day. Herbalife has something like 143mg per tablet which you take 4 times a day. The FDA wants regulations, but they can't because it's considered an herbal supplement. It scares me that people take this stuff. I know high school football players who take it so they can stay up after practice and study for their exams. The doctor who worked on my sister said he took it during his internship. Truck drivers take it. People just don't realize it can kill them. There was a woman on TV whose son was a salesman. He would travel all night to get to his destination. Right before he died, she said, "Honey, pull over if you get tired." He said, "Don't worry, Mom. I've got my pills. I'll be okay." About 5 minutes later, he had a massive stroke in front of his three-year old daughter." It's an asthma medication and shouldn't even be on the market for staying awake or weight loss. There needs to be some sort of legislation, but Herbalife and other companies keep fighting it.

The night before Melanie died, I said let's go down to PharMor. She said, "Oh, what the heck. Okay." That was odd because she never just picked up and went. I think I told her I loved her when she got out of the car. That bothers me—does she know that I loved her. She told me once that her husband hit her. I didn't do anything about it, because she said, "Don't you dare tell Mom and Dad. If you tell them, I won't speak to you ever again." Maybe if I had done something, she wouldn't have died. Not that he killed her, but maybe she could have taken better care of herself. Maybe she wouldn't have been so stressed out or so tired all the time. The last few years of her life were really shitty. He was so rotten to her; she wasn't happy.

Maybe I could have made a difference, if I had said something. But how do you force a grown woman to do anything? You don't. She did what she felt she needed to do. I regret that she can't see her son, Jake, grow up; that she can't raise him, because he's not being raised the way she would have wanted. We were on the phone right before she died. Melanie thought Jake might be at his grandmother's and said, "She needs to know Jake's my son, not hers." That was one of her last words. It haunts me, because I know she wouldn't want them raising her son.

I fought for him. Jake was in the car when his dad got a drunk driving ticket. We got a call at 3:00 in the morning. My dad and my husband had to go and get my nephew in Virginia. I fought and fought and fought with the social workers. They'd say, "He's not in immediate danger." What am I supposed to do? Be psychic and call when it's happening? There were rumors that his dad was a heroin user. I called child welfare and asked, "Can't you do something; can't you check him, because he's already on probation from a drunk driving charge?" All they did was call him and say, "Are you using heroin?" Like he's going to say, "Oh, yeah." Now he's in a methadone clinic to try to clean up.

It worries me, because I can't be with my nephew. I don't want him to be raised as a heathen. I don't want him to grow up and be one of those kids that nobody likes or has no morals or like a Columbine kid. I want him to grow up with manners, well cared for, to have a home, to know he's loved and not to think he's stupid. I'm not his biological mother. I'll never take the place of his mommy, but I want him to know there's a female figure that's always going to be there for him, who loves him. That my husband will be there, if he needs a father figure. Some place he's not going to be yelled at all the time. He lives just a few miles up the street. I usually get him every other week to watch him when his dad works. His dad's such a violent, mean, spiteful person. If I say one thing to him, like "I don't like this," then it would be, "You can't see him anymore." So it's a rock and a hard place.

I have everything on my shoulders. I have to be there for my mother. I have to deal with my brother-in-law. I worry about Jake, whether he gets to his doctors' appointments, his safety. I also have to raise my kids and be there for my husband. I have to be there for her friends. I don't think God puts anything more on you than you can handle. I think I'm handling it okay. Then there are days when I don't handle it very well, and there's nobody to say, "You've comforted me or you've been there for me, let me do the same for you."

I did get support from Tanya, a friend of Melanie's from her Grateful Dead days. They had lost touch because Tanya didn't like Melanie's new boyfriend. Tanya found out about Melanie's death the day we buried her. She called me, and we instantly bonded. It was wonderful because she knew Melanie as well as I did; she knew things that I didn't know from when I lived in Carolina. During the first three years especially, Tanya was very much there for me. She still is, but times are changing. She's going to college now and doesn't have as much time.

I went to see a therapist for a while about a year after Melanie died. I was sad and crying all the time. I wanted a miracle pill to get me out of my depression. They had me on Paxil at first. It was very tiring. I just didn't care about anything. Laundry could pile up to the ceiling, and I didn't care. I guess it did help for a while. I probably needed that at the time. It was hard to start talking to the therapist, but she was so nice.

I said, "When my mom lost her daughter, she lost her future. When you lose your sibling, you lose your past, your present, your future. That's the only person who knows everything about you. You're supposed to grow old with them. You're supposed to bury your parents. You're not supposed to bury your sister first. Melanie knew me better than anybody; she was my best friend. No matter how much you fight growing up or how much you disagree, that's the person who will back you up through anything. Then you lose her."

My family's never going to be how it was—ever. My parents are still living, but I'll never have my mom the way she was. Holidays are always going to be kind of strained. Things get overshadowed. Like my anniversary. I got married on Valentine's Day, and Melanie got married a year later on Valentine's Day. Instead of my mom saying, "Happy anniversary," she'll be depressed because that's Melanie's anniversary. Little things like that. I hope this doesn't sound selfish, but I need a mom, too. Just because Melanie died doesn't mean she stopped being my mom. I miss her, too, and I wish she could be back here. But Mom can't ignore me or ignore things I'm going through because she can't deal with it.

It's strange, but the second year is the worst. During the first year, you have memories of last year. You can say, "Remember last Christmas when she did this? Remember last Easter. Remember her last birthday." But that second year you have nothing. It gets better though. All of a sudden, you say, "Hey, I had a couple of good days." There's no specific time when it's like "Bam, I'm doing okay." You just gradually realize it's not as bad as it was. I still have some bad times. Her husband requested that they play a certain song at her funeral. It came on the radio the other day, and I just lost it.

I took my girlfriend to the hospital not long ago. I was in the waiting room and was doing okay. Then I saw a nurse usher a family into the little room. I kind of started not breathing well and freezing. I knew what was coming. I just wanted to scream as loud as I could. But I couldn't. I could hardly breathe. All of a sudden I started shaking. I saw the doctor, the same doctor that worked on my sister, and the nurse with the box of Kleenex behind her back, and I lost it. When I heard that woman wail, that was it. I threw down the book I was reading. I couldn't move. I couldn't sit up. I couldn't get out of there. I couldn't do anything. The bad moments just hit you.

I think that your body lets you handle only what you can handle. If it all hits you at one time, it would be the loony bin or you'd just shut down. When I was in counseling, I'd get to the point where I thought I'd break down and my body would shut it off. My counselor would say, "You get so close and then something happens. It triggers, and you shut off. Your body knows what you can handle." Maybe what happened that day at the hospital was something I couldn't let out the day my sister died.

The first time I had to go in and see the same doctor for my son, I was just bawling. He said, "Honey, I think it's just an ear infection." When I explained that my sister died and seeing him upset me, he remembered and it was okay.

I read in the paper that Compassionate Friends had sibling meetings at the hospital. I decided, "I've got to go to this meeting and be with other people." A lady saw me walking by and asked where I was going. I said to the sibling meeting. She said, "Honey, we haven't had that for a while, but you're more than welcome to come with me." They just took me in. They've been a godsend.

It helps to know I'm not alone, especially when I do off-the-wall stuff. Like one day, I couldn't find my keys. They were in the freezer. Four women said, "I do that, too." They make you feel like you're not going crazy. Everybody thinks it's a sob-fest, but it isn't. I get sad when new people come; that they need to come to the group. But you become a family, because all these people know what you're going through. You can call them anytime. I'd call a couple of the women, if I'd had a bad time with my mom, or I was really missing Melanie. They're there to listen. They're there for support.

People have a tendency to say, "Okay, it's been a year, you're done." Compassionate Friends say, "Hey, if it takes you ten years to be done, you're done then." There's no time limit on this. If you feel like going in and bawling your eyes out for a whole meeting, that's fine. If you want to vent all your anger, that's fine. It doesn't leave the room. They don't look at you like you're loony. They've all been through it. Being with parents has been good, because I think I've helped them. In a way being in the group, you're helping yourself, because you're helping somebody else; even if it's just to hug somebody. A lot of people in the group have other adult children and didn't realize that some of their decisions might be hurtful. For example, parents might not want to celebrate Christmas, but that might hurt their other children. We discuss things like that. Sometimes they'll ask me, "How would you feel about this?" I get a lot out of that group. It's nice to know I have a place to go where nobody judges me or looks at me funny. We laugh a lot. We have some good times, and we have some really bad times. Everybody is just there for each other.

You've got to let yourself grieve. I know that it hurts. Nobody wants to cry, and it's horrible. If you don't let yourself grieve, then that's where you get problems. There were times when I went and lay on her grave because I missed her so much. I had to cry. Afterward, I'd feel better. I'll go through her things periodically, because I need to touch something of hers or smell something of hers. If you don't let yourself do it, then you're doing a disservice to yourself. I'll miss her all my life. I'll probably cry when I'm 50 years old, because I miss her.

It was hard for my husband. I'd say, "Don't touch me." I wanted a hug, but I didn't want a hug. I wanted to be alone, but I didn't want to be alone. At that time, I didn't really know what I wanted. There's nothing anybody can do. My daughter would ask, "Why's Mommy crying, Daddy?" He would explain that I was sad because of Melanie. He's never said anything like, "You need to stop this. It's been this long." He just let me do what I needed to do. That's the best thing—to let people do what they need to do, as long as they're not hurting themselves.

I've always wondered if it was hard for my husband, because he tried to resuscitate her and couldn't. He's never really said how it affected him. They were close. They'd goof off with each other and pick on each other all the time. So I'm sure it affected him,

Some women have been going to Compassionate Friends for ten years and they still have what we call the big roller coaster ride. You have periods of good and bad and good and bad. Sometimes you'll feel really good and think you don't deserve it. At first, it's, "I'm happy, but I shouldn't be happy, because I've had this most horrible thing happen to me." It does get better. Then you hear a song, or smell a perfume. Melanie used to wear patchouli perfume. Sometimes I'll smell it and it makes me sad; other times it makes me really happy, because it was a part of her.

I do birthday parties for Melanie. Some people probably think that's morbid, but I figure that the more people who have a memory of her, she will never be gone. For her birthday, I just go all out. The anniversary of her death is rougher. That's not a party day for me. It's a quiet day. I usually go up and sit with her for a while and talk with her. Her birthday is different. It just came to me. How could I let this go by? Everybody was, "Yeah, we need to do that." We've done it every year since she's died. We invite her friends, my husband, my family, her ex-sister-in-law, her ex-brother-in-law. Her husband never comes, but her mother-in-law does. Everybody brings their kids. Even people who didn't know her will come. Melanie's ex-sister-in-law brought her new boyfriend. He came and spent the day with us. That was so amazing, because he didn't know her, and he didn't think we were crazy.

Her best friend, her sister-in-law and I wear her perfume the day of her birthday party. We all wear tie dye or the hippiest clothes we can find. I have a list of the songs that we play all day. We start at the grave. Last year, we had poppers; we popped confetti everywhere. We did what I call "heaven balloons." Everybody tied a message they wanted her to have to a balloon. Her son told me what to write, "I miss you, mommy. I love you." We released them. They all went up; none broke. They went up as high as you could see. It was just the biggest feeling of awe. Then we lit candles on her grave. The first year, we didn't know when her husband was going to get her headstone up. But it was there for her birthday. So we lit candles, and they all went out at the same time. They stayed out for 7 seconds, and then they all came back up. They weren't trick candles. They were regular candles. I get a cake. We go to her favorite place, which is Ohiopyle and have a picnic. Everybody gets her flowers. I always get a coral rose to throw in the water. She always wanted me to go there. She'd say, "You've got to go up to Ohiopyle, Terry.

It's beautiful. Hiking. The mountains. Everything is gorgeous." I never did it when she was alive. So we go and celebrate her day. It's usually a really good day, not a lot of tears. People tell stories, "Remember when she did this; remember when she did that?"

Last year was kind of hard planning it. I thought, "This is stupid, I quit." But I couldn't quit, because I know she's up there saying, "Look what they're doing for me." The day Melanie died, I told my mom, "I don't ever want to be afraid to talk about her." I talk about her every chance I get. I talk to her son. "Your mommy used to do this; your mommy used to do that." We'll plant flowers around the tombstone or hang a special ornament on the tree for her. The more I try to do things in her memory or let people know about her, the more it helps. Then she's not truly gone. As long as nobody forgets, she'll never, ever be gone. As long as people keep coming, I'll keep having her birthday party. I'll have it by myself if I have to.

What makes me angry is people who don't know how lucky they are. My one girl friend won't talk to her brother. She says horrible things about him. I'm thinking, "You have one. Be thankful you have someone." I'm alone. Melanie was my only sibling. I want to shake her and say, "Be thankful, because they could go any time, any day, any minute. You never know."

I'm not super religious; not a Bible-toting, go-to-church-every-Sunday person. We have Bible study here every once in a while. I believe there's a God; I believe what he wrote. Since her death, I've become more spiritual. I believe He did take her for a reason. That everybody does have a time. It's not a fluke. You're here for your amount of time and then it's time for you to go. I believe it is a much better place where they go. I'm becoming more spiritual as far as the world around me. Trying to be more like Melanie was. Give everybody a break. Try not to hate the world, try not to hate everybody; try to be more forgiving and understanding.

I would hate to believe there's nothing after this. That she's just lying there; just rotting. That would be horrible. The Jehovah Witnesses got me right after she died. They would come to the house. I had just had my baby, and I needed anybody who would talk to me. Then they started saying you just lie there. They believe you don't rise till He comes to get you. I didn't want to hear that. She's not just lying in dirt. She's not just a pile of dirt, either.

I know some people don't agree with me, but we do get signs. Even a lot of preachers I've talked to, agree that your loved ones will send you signs. You just have to be open to it. The day we buried Melanie was bright and sunny. We were at the casket and I looked up. A white butterfly flew over the casket. For one minute, I smiled, then thought, "Why am I smiling?" I saw this butterfly, and it was almost like she was saying, "I'm okay. Don't worry about me." Whenever I have a rotten day, or something horrible happens, or I really need her, that butterfly is always there. I found a beautiful, white, net butterfly and always put it on my Christmas tree for Melanie.

My son was diagnosed with a kidney problem. It's not where it should be. We didn't know if he had one or if it was functioning. We had to go to Children's Hospital—in the middle of smog-filled Oakland where nothing lives. As we were leaving, a white butterfly flew past my window. I knew he was going to be okay. I knew she was with me. I don't think the butterfly is her, but that is her message to me that "I'm with you."

My daughter remembers her Aunt Melanie very well, even though she was only 2 ½ years old when Melanie died. On her first day of pre-school, a white butterfly came, flew between her legs, flew around her head, around her arms.

The Thanksgiving after we lost Melanie was cold. I was sitting outside having a cigarette, really missing her, and crying. I said, "Just get your stinking butt down here for one second so I can know you're okay." Out of nowhere, this white butterfly went right past me. It's very odd, how our loved ones give us signals.

Melanie loved ice skating. Tanya got tickets for us to see Tara Lipinski, and I knew Melanie would have loved it. I said to Tanya, "I wonder if Melanie's here." Just then Tara Lipinski turned around right in front of me, and she had a big white butterfly in her hair. I knew Melanie was there.

I didn't know it, but a butterfly is the Compassionate Friends' symbol. When I was walking into the hospital, I saw a plaque in the shape of a butterfly and knew I was supposed to be there. There was a dedication ceremony for a mural they had painted. They had triangular boxes for the kids to open and release butterflies. One would not leave me alone. It flew all up and down me. I bawled my eyes out.

My mom and I went to see TV psychic John Edward when he was in Pittsburgh. I'm kind of torn, because the Bible says you shouldn't believe in soothsayers, and you shouldn't believe in people who say they can talk to the dead. I'm a Christian so I should believe that. But part of me is so desperate for any kind of contact with Melanie that I'm thinking, "Why does it have to be the devil's work? Why can't God give somebody the power to talk to someone and do good?" John Edward doesn't tell you rotten things. However, I got really mad. He was reading me, but didn't know it. He said an older woman, grandmotherly figure; the name sounds like "L. Lewis." He's never wrong with the first letter. I have an Aunt Lois. Somebody fell or had gotten hurt at an amusement park but didn't die. My aunt had fallen off the top of a Ferris wheel when she was young. That's me; I know it's me. He said, "No it's the couple behind you." But they never got it. I was very upset with him. I cried and haven't watched him since.

The night before we saw John Edward, Mom and I went to a wedding. The next day she called and asked, "What did you put in my purse?" I said, "Cigarettes and money." She asked, "Were there any butterflies at the wedding?" "No. None on the tables." Mom had found a white confetti butterfly at the bottom of her purse, even though she had cleaned it out before putting her stuff in. We had been wondering, "Can Melanie see us at this wedding? Is she with us?" Then my mom found the butterfly.

So they do give you signs. A family at the grief group had lost their only daughter. Their daughter loved money. They began to find nickels at her grave; then all over the house—in their shoes, under their pillows. Weird places. It was like their daughter's signal to them. Another lady's daughter loved music and played it all the time when she was home. Now the stereo comes on. Her mom unplugged it; it would still come on. She packed it in a box; put it in the attic; it would still come on. So they do send you signals and let you know you're not alone. I do believe Melanie watches me. I feel her presence.

My son was born three months after Melanie died, but she named him. We had put Cameron Dean on his birth certificate. But I kept calling him Gabe. My husband said, "What are you calling him that for? That's not what we named him." I had no idea. I prayed to her the night before we brought him home. I said, "Melanie, I'm in a bad spot. I don't know what's going on. What do you want me to name him? You have to let me know by morning. I have to know beyond a shadow of a doubt." When I woke up, I called my husband and said, "Look, come early. We've got to fill out a new birth certificate. Melanie called him something else. That's what she wants me to name him."

Other weird things have happened. Her Dead Head boyfriend was in Maine with his new girlfriend the day Melanie died. He told me, "We were in a tent. I woke up and Melanie was standing there. Just looking as gorgeous as the first day we met. I'm thinking, 'How in the heck did she find me up here in the midst of all this.' I just sat there; I knew I wasn't dreaming it. She sort of faded away." When he came home, he learned she had died. He had no way of knowing. It's like she went to say good-bye.

Once when we were going to North Carolina to visit my husband's family I was wearing a shirt that my daughter had no way of knowing was Melanie's. About 4:00 in the morning, Kylie woke up and said, "Mommy, Aunt Melanie said that's okay. She doesn't need her clothes any more."

Then once we were coming back from my obstetrician and my mom was in the car. Kylie kept saying, "Melanie came down. Aunt Melanie." I'm ignoring her, because I don't want my mom to cry. She repeated herself three times, so finally I said, "What do you mean Aunt Melanie came down?" "Mommy, Jake is really sick.

He's at Grandma's. He's sick. She's sitting with him." When I got home, I called. Jake had a 105 temperature and was sick as a dog. Kylie had no way of knowing this.

People who believe, people like John Edward, say that children's minds are so clean and open and not yet tarnished by the world that they're closer to spiritual energy. John Edward says that a lot of times they let you know through electricity. My windshield wipes will flip on and off. I've had them checked three times. They cannot find the reason why they do this. I'll say, "Mel, stop it already." And they'll quit.

I know now that my family isn't invincible. My friend lost three brothers. A woman at Compassionate Friends lost two children at different times. It can happen again. That's my biggest fear. It can happen at any time. I've noticed since Melanie died, I constantly fear everything. Before, I was just scared for her. Now I'm scared about everything. I don't like being scared about everything, all the time.

I have a fear for my mother. If she leaves the house and I hear a siren, I freak. If my husband's not home at a certain time, I freak. If a friend leaves, I freak. There was a time I thought I would throw up whenever I heard a siren, and the fire house is just up the road.

My daughter went for tonsil and adenoid surgery. The doctor missed the bleeding disorder that she has. Her regular pediatrician found it. For a whole week before her surgery I threw up, because I just knew she was going to bleed to death on the table and that was all there was to it. I just have irrational fears. My husband can be five minutes late from work and I'm afraid he wrecked. Or something on the car can blow up, and it's like oh, my life's going to end. The fearfulness bothers me. I hope it will change. I pray about it. I try to work on it, but it's hard. It's like I'm telling my body and brain, it's enough. Stop it, stop it, stop it. Everything's going to be okay. But that fearfulness goes its own way. I thought I had so much power being at home, taking care of Melanie. I found out that I have diddly squat power. So it's really scary now.

For a while I would dream about Melanie, and that was kind of hard. Then I had one where I was touching her. I was probably touching myself, but I could swear I was touching her arms. We were in a beautiful field and she looked beautiful. I was bawling, but she was laughing like she would do. She said, "Quit crying. Quit crying. I'm fine." I said, "I miss you so bad, Melanie. I can't believe I'm touching you." She said, "Terry, I'm fine. Just know everything is okay. Everything's fine." Then she just kind of looked over her shoulder and said, "Well, I have to go now." I said, "No, no. You can't." She said, "I'm okay. Don't worry about me." I really haven't had a dream about her since then. I think they let you know that they're okay.

11

TINA and LISA

Tina is one of six children—3 boys and 3 girls. She and Lisa are in the middle, with an older sister and three younger brothers. Tina is 4 years younger than Lisa who died at age 47.

My mother had a major stroke which incapacitated her. She couldn't walk, swallow, could only talk a little. Mainly because Lisa wanted to, we brought our mother home instead of sending her to a nursing home. Her care fell mostly on Lisa, because they lived together. So for three or four months, Lisa took care of Mom; we all helped out, but she did the most of it. Then Mom was in and out of the hospital. When she died, Lisa probably felt it the most. She had been taking care of Mom, and then there was nothing. She had never married; had no children. Also, she didn't have a lot of money. She worked as a school secretary. She and Mom supported each other. Without my mom's income, she had financial problems. We all tried to help out, but it wasn't easy.

We found Lisa dead on New Year's Day. She had invited my husband, my daughter and me for dinner. I called once during the morning. I was working on lesson plans and didn't think anything of it when she didn't answer. I thought she was doing laundry or something and didn't hear the phone. We were going to go at 2:00. I called about 1:00. She still didn't answer, and I was getting concerned. I called my brother and my niece. Neither one of them had heard from her. My husband, daughter and I went right over. The door was locked, so I used my key, but the chain was on. I could see her on the sofa through the crack in the door. She was white and very still. We broke the door down. The coroner said that she had died about 6:30 in the morning, but we think it was closer to New Year's Eve. She hadn't smoked any cigarettes in the morning which she usually did. The bed was made, and I doubt she had gotten up and made it. But those were just feelings and there was no reason to argue with him, so we just let it ride. She had a cerebral aneurysm. They said she was probably having severe headaches. That was another reason we thought that she wouldn't have made the bed and cleaned up everything.

I was very close to Lisa; closer than with my other siblings. We lived less than a mile and a half away from each other. If she wanted to go shopping, she'd call me. If I wanted to go shopping, I'd call her. We'd always go out together. My other sister had her family since she was 21 or 22; she was always doing things with them. Also, I would go a lot to help with my mom, so I was close to Lisa, because of that. When mom was in and out of the hospital, we'd go together to visit her. We were extremely close.

Her death brought the rest of us closer. Lisa died without a will. We had to pull together to sort everything out. When my father died, my mom had put the house in Lisa and my one brother's names, because at the time they didn't have a place of their own. A lot fell on my brother, because the house was his. We had to give him power of attorney. Lisa was a collector; we're still going through stuff. Last November, my one sister-in-law invited us for dinner. I don't recall that happening before. Just about a month ago, we had everybody here. We're pulling together a little more. We all felt shocked that it happened; it could happen to any of us. We need to make the most of what time we have.

There has been a little lessening of the grief, but I feel like there is a hole in my life. At certain times, it really hits me again. Shopping is still hard for me. I don't like to go by myself. My other sister doesn't live that close and she's pretty busy, so I don't usually like to call her. I have two adult daughters who are in college. When they come home, they do go shopping with me. Lisa's death made my husband extremely solicitous. He and I are not of the same faith, but he started attending church with me every Sunday. For the week and a half after Lisa died, he didn't leave my side. I finally had to say, "I just need some time by myself."

Religion has given me a sense of solace. I attend church very regularly. My other sister is pretty active in the church so we see each other there. That is a bond for us. I tend to listen a lot to the hymns. I teach kindergarten and use music a lot in teaching. It is something that I turn to a lot.

New Year's Day was hard this year. I called my one brother and said, "I don't want to be home. Let's do something." We took everyone to a local hotel that had a New Year's Day buffet. Christmas was also a little hard. We do a gift exchange where each Christmas we draw names for the next year. We had drawn names a week before she died; I had her name. When I was going through her things, I found the name that she had drawn. I just switched the names. I think we're going to continue that tradition. We get together for other holidays and for a lot of summer picnics. I think we'll try to keep these traditions the same as much as possible.

Her birthday was hard last year. One of the teachers from my school sent me a really nice card on my sister's birthday. For my mom, we take flowers to the cemetery. My younger brother has been really good about checking at the cemetery, making sure everything's okay. Last summer we all got together and planted a dogwood tree at the grave, because she loved dogwoods. On certain holidays, we've donated flowers to decorate the sanctuary in memory of Lisa, Mom, and Dad.

Lisa was very opinionated. She loved clothes. She dressed very well. She was a school secretary and was extremely organized. She ran the school, not the principal. She was like a drill sergeant. If they didn't have their forms in when they were supposed to, she'd tell them about it. Actually, that was another thing that made us close, because we worked in the same district.

The school where she worked is still dealing with it. She had worked there for 18 years, knew all the kids. Between her viewing and the funeral service over 400 people came. Many were students she had worked with. The superintendent came. There were a lot of nice comments. I got a lot of cards. That was nice, touching. The community where the school is located arranged for the state police to come and guide us to the cemetery. Kids came in with music. The school organized a site visit for the students so that teachers could come to the service. The principal is setting up a little courtyard memorial at the school.

Not long after she died, the teachers went on strike, had marches, and other group actions. I didn't want to go, because I'd see teachers from her building and people who would ask about her. Now I run into them occasionally, but not a lot, because she was in a different school. There are times when it is hard. Whenever anyone mentions her school, I think about her.

The funeral director was wonderful. His son was in kindergarten at the school where my sister worked. He also knew her because of my mom. He really helped a lot. We knew that they'd have to do an autopsy. We didn't know what she had died of. We thought maybe a heart attack. They ask questions, like, "Was she taking any drugs? Was she depressed?" Those questions can upset you, because you know where they're leading. That was unsettling. We never had any contact with the police or coroner after they took her away. The funeral director handled everything. He told us the results of the autopsy.

We met with the funeral director and had gotten everything organized, ordered the casket, made all the arrangements. My niece was there, and after the funeral director left, she said, "I think Aunt Lisa wanted to be cremated." All of a sudden we went, "Oh, yes, she did." We called the funeral director, and he said, "That's not a problem. We'll still do the viewing because of so many people, but we'll just change to a wooden casket."

Because my mom had died so recently, Lisa had said she wanted to be cremated, but we really didn't talk about any other preferences she might have. Her favorite color was black so that helped us to decide what outfit to put on her. As a matter of fact, the casket was black. We come from an Irish background. When we talked with the minister about the service, we included Irish poetry that she loved and the Celtic cross. We read an Irish blessing and told anecdotes about her.

Not being able to say good-bye has been a problem for me. I keep thinking that I should have gone over the night before, because she was alone. My brother who lived at the house had gone to Baltimore with his girl friend. My husband and I went to the first night celebration on New Year's Eve. She was by herself, and I feel guilty about that. My sister-in-law is a nurse, and I asked, "Is there something we should have picked up on to know that this was coming?" I asked my doctor about it. They said, "No." Still, I should have gone over to make sure she was okay. I wish that I could have said good-bye.

Lisa was not one to go to the doctor very much. That's one of the things I've learned. Not to let that slide. My husband turned 50 just before Lisa died. I really pushed him to go for a check-up. I was having headaches, so I talked those over with my doctor. My dad had had an aneurysm; in his chest, not his brain. When I asked whether it was hereditary, the doctor said, "It can be." He told me some things I can do if I ever want to get it checked. I not sure if I'd even want to know. If my brothers and sister have problems, they get it checked out.

I have a very strong faith. I believe that my parents and my sister have gone to a better place. Although I miss her, I can't wish that she would be here or in pain. I knew that she would never want to go through what my mom went through.

I guess I do have some anxiety since this happened. The events of September 11 compounded that. I cry much more now. I hardly ever used to cry. Now news stories make me cry. The whole issue of not going out shopping. It's much easier just to stay at home with things that comfort me. This summer I had some serious health problems. I have asthma and was having a lot of difficulty breathing. I thought everything that had happened—my sister, the strike at school—was causing the asthma to kick up. It turns out it wasn't asthma, but a thyroid problem that was causing a very rapid heartbeat. Getting to the doctor and getting that straightened out helped a little bit. But really, I didn't go anywhere this summer; I didn't do anything. Another thing is that my husband and I are having our 25th anniversary this summer. For the last three or four years, we've planned a trip to Hawaii. Lisa was going to go with us. Now I don't want to go. In the past, Lisa had come with us to the shore and on a Disney cruise. She had done a lot of vacations with us and I didn't want to go without her.

I guess it helps to talk about it. Having religious faith helps a lot. Keeping my family close. My younger brother still lives in the house that they owned together. We talk a lot, not a lot about Lisa, but once in a while. I can talk about it with my older sister and my husband. I have a co-worker whose mother died not long ago. We talk a lot. The wife of our minister works with me. She and I talk quite a bit; mostly about life and the hereafter. I've always believed that there is life after death. When my father died, I said it would be a lot harder if I didn't believe that there was something afterward.

In terms of any final thoughts, I'd just emphasize how important the role of the funeral director is. He was able to tell us about things that we never thought of. Because he knew Lisa, he knew we would need to have an evening viewing. Now days, a lot of people will just have a viewing right before the service, but he said, "There are going to be a lot of people. You're going to have to have an evening viewing." So he really took us through that process and helped us make the arrangements in the least painful way. You know, there are so many practical things to take care of after a death. You just have to deal with those step by step. It's what helps you get through it.

12

MARION and TED

Marion is the youngest of three children. She is 16 years younger than her sister who is a nun and 12 years younger than her brother, Ted, who died in 1989 at age 55. In 1947, when Marion was two, her sister left to join the convent. Her father died that same year. Her mother never remarried.

My mother was a widow, but was very active in the community. She worked as a cook for the nuns so she could take me with her. Every Wednesday night she went bowling, and Ted was my baby sitter. He was a teenager, so I got to hang out at the dairy bar with him and his friends. To this day I have a really close relationship with many of those guys. They'd do these terrible adolescent things, like pretend they were hitting Ted to make me cry. I remember walking home and Ted would say, "I wish you were a boy." He taught me to drive. That was our relationship, not a father figure, just a fun big brother; my protector.

I was more of my mother's constant companion. Ted gave her a bit of a run around. He'd get into trouble with his studies. But my mother was definitely in charge of the house. He had an incredible closeness with and respect for my mother. When he graduated from high school, he went into the trades and became a brick layer. While he was doing an apprenticeship, he was drafted into the army toward the end of the Korean War. They shipped him to Japan. He wasn't in battle, but he minded very much being so far away. Having him so far away was a real adjustment for my mother and me. He just stayed in the army for two years, then came home and married.

When Ted got married, he moved in with my mom and me and we lived together until I left home at 18. His wife was like a big sister to me. I was close to his five children; the oldest two are like my siblings. I would often find myself explaining him to them, because he was so gruff. He had a heart of gold, but he was very gruff. They would misinterpret him. He was very honest and that was hard on his kids, especially when they were adolescents. As they got older they understood that he was just gruff.

We went to all family activities. Ted was the heart and soul of the family reunions; made sure everybody got together. He'd have an open house on Christmas day night. He'd have a big buffet, and everyone would come, no one was excluded. He was close to lots of cousins, nieces, nephews, aunts and uncles. He would also do repairs for the older aunts and uncles and never take money. My one aunt would show you everything he did in her house and say, "He'd never take a penny, but I'd try to sneak it to his wife." Often on Sundays he'd get up, go to mass, come back and make breakfast for Mom. He was very kind.

Right after I moved into the duplex where I now live, it went up for sale. Ted bought it and became my landlord. He kept his scaffolds and tools in the big garage behind it. He'd always be up early on Saturday and would come over to work on little jobs, fixing things at his house or mine. I'd make coffee; we'd sit and talk about issues in the family. That's when we began to develop our adult friendship. We could argue. We were very different. He was very controlling; in some ways a very traditional Italian man. One of our biggest fights happened when my best friend got married and kept her own name.

We remained in close proximity throughout his life. Our relationship grew into mutual respect. He would ask my opinion and discuss different issues, especially about his kids. I'll never forget discussing cars with him. His daughter wanted to buy a Honda, and

Ted told her to buy an automatic. I said, "If you're going to buy an automatic, you really ought to buy American." At the time the Japanese were making good stick shifts, but not good automatic transmissions. He looked at me and asked, "How do you know that." I told him where I read it and said, "You can read about anything you want to know about." He hadn't been much of a reader, but then he started reading. He said, "I'm going to find out about a lot of stuff." I think he was amazed that I had knowledge about something just because I had read about it.

I was the first woman on both sides of the family to go to college. Ted made it possible, because he helped me financially. My grades went home. I didn't think he noticed, but other people would say, "Hey, your brother told me you got a 4.0." He very much wanted all of his children to go to school. Then he started taking lifelong learning classes at community college.

I wish I would have told him how proud I was of him. I don't think he ever knew how much I valued him. I hope he knew. I remember right after he died I wanted to tell him that I wished it was me and not him. One night I dreamed I told him that, and it gave me such relief. I dreamed about him four or five times. It was so nice. I didn't even mind waking up and knowing it was a dream, because I'd actually been having a conversation with him.

Although he was a bricklayer, I thought with some encouragement, he could have gone to college. He could read blueprints. When he was allowed to be creative, he'd put little designs in different places on a building. He was very talented that way. It makes me feel good to pass those buildings, like the shiny red Chinese restaurant on McKee Place; he built that. We go and look at that beautiful brickwork.

By the time he died, he was a bricklayer for the county. He'd realized that he needed to get into a job with benefits and a pension. He was foreman on a job where the county was adding a new wing to a building that used to be a juvenile justice hall. He had a bad headache when he went to work on Monday morning. He complained a couple of times to a friend on the job that his head really, really hurt. At lunch he bent over and had a massive heart attack. He was dead on arrival at the hospital.

My dad had died of a massive heart attack when he was 42, and his father had died of a heart attack. Ted doctored for that. He would go for stress tests, for cholesterol tests. He'd had a physical a month or two before he died. Cholesterol levels were okay. Stress test was okay. Then he just had this massive heart attack.

It's comforting to know he went so quickly, because he was such an active person he wouldn't have handled being sick. But the shock was great. It took me three years to get through the shock. I wrecked my car shortly after he died. A car was coming, and I just pulled out into an intersection. I never saw the car. I didn't know anything about the accident. I felt like a spectator for the longest time. I'd be somewhere and feel like I was watching. I'd get so angry with people who were having a good time. People would invite me to a party, and I would think, "Don't they know what I'm feeling." Part of the anger was having no closure. As hard as it is to watch someone who's sick, you have time to say everything you want to say. That was really a life learning lesson for me—to say everything I want to say to everybody I care about.

We had him laid out in our community. It was February and was freezing cold and sleeting. But the lines went out the funeral home door, all through the parking lot, up the street,. There were hundreds and hundreds of people; people he had befriended. He was a bricklayer, not a politician; he was an unassuming man. It was pretty amazing.

After he died, I'd be angry with him. He and his wife were planning his daughter's wedding. He was beginning to know that two of his sons were in the early stages of having trouble with drugs. So I was angry that he left me with these things to deal with. His wife is very kind, very sweet, but she's definitely not a leader, definitely doesn't take charge. Her way of coping is pretending it's not happening. Plus she was going through her own adjustment. She'd say, "My whole life changed and I had nothing to say about it." My mother was still living and it was hard for her because they had been so close. We were all dealing with the loss. I had truly lost a friend and a partner in the family situation. My sister is a nun and was not involved with anything going on in the family. Ted and I had shared those kinds of responsibilities and now it was up to me.

For three years after Ted died, I took his oldest son to rehab. He's ten years clean and sober. His new addiction is running and biking; he's so healthy. He now owns the building where I live. His business has taken off. We're incredibly close. I know Ted would be very proud of him. Unfortunately, Ted's youngest son still has a drug problem and, I think, some mental health problems. I suspect a lot of it is guilt over the relationship that he and his dad had over those last couple of years. Ted had realized something was wrong and was being very hard on him; was getting ready to kick him out of the house. I can't reach the youngest one.

In addition to the buildings Ted worked on, my strongest sense of his legacy comes from his children and grandchildren. His daughter looks like him; she has his personality; the fieriness; the flame up, then everything is okay after a minute or so. I see him in his grandchildren's behaviors and interests. I went to *The Nutcracker* and was so sad because he loved to sing. He sang all the time—in the shower, in the church choir; he thought he was Frank Sinatra. I was watching his grandson on stage with all this beautiful music. He would have been so moved and proud to have one of his grandchildren be involved in that type of activity.

His legacy is also the impact he had on people's lives. People still talk about what he gave to them. One night Ted's daughter was at a school meeting and introduced herself to some other parents. When she mentioned that her dad grew up on St. Claire Street and mentioned his name, one of the men said, "Not, Teddy—we were buddies. We were such good buddies. He was always so neat." (He was compulsively neat for being a contractor.) He said, "He was so kind. He was just the nicest guy. We hung out as teenagers. Even as a young boy, he was so responsible." It was important for my niece to be connected to that part of her dad's life. The way he touched people's lives was probably his greatest legacy.

I have some photographs that I value, but stuff is not important to me. Memories are important. I can't get over when people argue over things. After Mom died I gave her stuff away; I gave her jewelry to her granddaughters. I cherish things that she gave me while she was alive. She gave me this ring. It's not even that valuable. When she was 20 years old, she was in my godmother's wedding. The best man bought this ring as a bridesmaid gift. She had it cut off her finger because she had very bad arthritis, and I asked if I could have it. So things like this that she actually handed to me are important. The same with my brother. The last Christmas gift he gave me was a dress watch. I wear it for all special occasions and at holiday time. Things he gave me before he died are meaningful.

I want to keep his memory alive for his kids and his grandkids. I try to have a memorial mass for him and my mother the Sunday between Christmas and New Year's, because everybody's home. We all go to mass and the little ones serve on the altar. Then we have brunch. It's an annual celebration of their lives. That's important for the history of the family. We write down stories that his children and grandchildren don't know. My oldest nephew is astounded when I tell him stories about his dad. There's a house for sale in our neighborhood and he said it's such a great house. I said, "Your dad almost bought it before he bought the one you grew up in." Their mother can't do that; she's never gotten to the point where she can function okay. If you don't celebrate the memories, you've lost them completely. Fortunately, I got over the part where I was angry at everything. I didn't do Thanksgiving; no celebrations; nothing. Then it was an awakening. He's not coming back. Now I want people to know everything good about him.

There are still a lot of mournful moments. I continue to miss him, because there are constantly new things that I want him to be there for. Well, even the duplex where I live. Nothing remained broken for even an hour. Not only was it fixed, it was excellent. He was a perfectionist. There are so many little things we depended on him for and no one has taken his place. I've never had another relationship that comes close to it. It's been 12 years, but the loss is still fresh; I still grieve. Like the holidays—we don't do anything like we used to. We don't go to his house. When we get together, it's at his daughter's house or my house. It's just too hard to go to the family house.

My relationship with my sister is very different from Ted's and mine. She left home to become a nun when she was 18. She would come for short visits, so she never got involved in the hard, day-to-day things. Ted's and my life continued together. We were both so independent. We talked about her one time and he said, "She's always been a cry baby. She would whine and complain about everything." I'm not sure if she ever regretted becoming a nun. Eighteen is so young to make a decision like that. She really wanted it; my father really wanted it. He was helping her prepare and was very proud of her. They thought it would work out really well. But she's always been a pretty negative person. Part of her health problems now may be depression. She may feel the loss of family connection. Now we're close in the sense that I call her weekly to make sure she's okay. It's more of a caring thing. It's not like a friendship; we have nothing in common.

When I was 18, I wanted to join the Peace Corps, but my mother wouldn't hear of it. So I went to the convent instead. Needless to say, it didn't work out. I had all this energy. I wanted to do good in the world. All through high school I had circles of friends that were all different—school friends, summer friends from the street, friends from some of the rougher Pittsburgh neighborhoods. I did a lot of volunteer work; was active in the Red Cross. Based on all my volunteer experience I thought that joining the convent would give me the opportunity to help people. That was a mistake. I found myself living with a bunch of self-serving women who were driving me crazy.

I was shocked. I thought nuns were generous, giving women. When I entered, I became one of the people who waited on the sisters. We served them meals; cleaned their rooms. They ordered us around. They'd ring a bell if they wanted something brought to the dining room. I did stick it out for three and a half years. For two of the years, I was taking college classes. When I went to the convent, Ted was so upset he couldn't talk about it. He was just beside himself. His oldest two kids had a really hard time with it, because I was the one who took them ice skating and swimming; taught them how to ride bikes. When I came out he gave me a big party. At one point he told me, "I really don't wish that you were a boy."

Ted's death didn't really change my religious beliefs. My religion is very personal. It was a comfort to think about heaven and God; to think of my mother greeting my brother; that they're all somewhere probably playing cards with my uncles, because that's what they always did when they got together. My church family was a comfort; the people are very caring. A lot of them were friends with my brother, because he would go to my church for special events. I found that comforting. I didn't have thoughts like, "God took him," or "why did He do this to us?" I don't think of a powerful being like that. Things happen, and I'm not sure anyone is in control of them. Religion did give me comfort to the point that I continued to pick up his grandchildren and take them to church with me when they were little. Of course, being the social people that we are, the big thing about going to church was after mass. We'd have brunch at a friend's house, and the kids would play. Maybe the comfort comes from all the holiday traditions connected to the church. Like the Christmas party started with mass on Christmas morning and then went on from there. Ted's daughter who lives closest to me has three children. Not long ago, she joined my church. She said it's comfortable being there with family, because that's what we always did. She feels connected to her dad through the church.

Ted's death definitely changed my view of life. Because I was so young when my dad died, I wondered what would happen to me if my mother would die. I had lots of aunts and uncles who helped to take care of me, like if my mother had to go to the hospital. I would think that if my mother died, I'd go to live with one of my aunts, and that gave me a sense of security, Maybe that's why I'm the kind of aunt I am. With my brother, it changed my priorities.

I decided to enter a doctoral program after Ted died and my mother was failing. I needed something to keep my mind occupied so I started taking courses. Mom would be in the hospital and sleep for hours. I'd take whatever I'd need for a project, and spread my papers all over her bed. She'd wake up and say, "What is all this stuff." I got into the doctoral program, because I needed to compensate for the sense of loss. Yet, I remember wondering, "Will I die before it's finished?" That's one of the reasons it was so difficult to put so much time into the dissertation. I fought it for so long, because I thought, "What if I die? What if I die next month? Would I want to spend all of this time writing or would I want to spend all of this time with people who are important to me?"

I face life very differently now. I don't put things or people off. I was going to travel every month, but 9/11 has me a wreck. I'm sort of building up the courage for a trip to Italy in the fall. That was going to be my reward if I ever finished the doctorate. I think about other things, like what would it be like if Ted was still here? We would probably talk about getting a place in Florida, even if we wouldn't be there at the same time. We were both interested in traveling. I had gone to Italy several years before he died. When I saw the Parthenon and all those other great buildings, I wished he could be there, because he would have appreciated the architecture and the construction; how these buildings are still standing after all these years. He never got to do that.

I wonder if there is ever going to be a time when I can talk about him and not tear up. My doctor said, "You really should think about a group." She had asked me some specific questions about my mother or Ted and I teared up. She said, "It doesn't seem like you've resolved that." That turned me off. I don't want to resolve losing him. The grief is usually triggered by conversation. For a long time it was triggered if I saw a blue pick-up truck, because that's what he drove to work. It was triggered at *The Nutcracker* with the little one on stage, or something special that my niece's children do that he would have liked. Going into a group really repels me, because the other people didn't know him. It would take me so much time to deal with the personalities. Intellectually I know that a group would probably help, but I don't want to do it that way. I want to grieve the way I'm doing it. It keeps him alive for me. In my family, tears aren't an embarrassment; they're a sign of respect. It gets cumbersome, because you can't talk while you're tearing up. But it's not something to hide or be embarrassed about.

About three years after Ted died, my mother died. I think that brought everything full circle. Until then, I was still going to the house a lot, being in his house, being around everything of his. I found some comfort in that, but after Mom passed away it was like a phase of my life was over. I moved on, but it took a long time to feel normal. I had known death of uncles, aunts, and cousins, but losing my only brother was the most unique, most profound, experience of my life.

13

MAY and BRAD

May is the 12ᵗʰ of 13 children. Brad, the fourth oldest, was about 14 years older than May. He died in 1993 at the age of 58.

Brad's heart had been damaged when he had rheumatic fever as a child. The year before he died, he had open heart surgery and then got an infection in the heart. That was really serious. His idea of taking care of himself did not match the doctor's advice. He was involved in a Boy Scout camp where he had to go up and down this big hill. His idea of taking it easy the summer after his surgery was riding a golf cart up and down that hill. He did not give up the camp. He did not cut his hours back. There were other things he was supposed to have done, but he didn't. He spent August at Temple University Hospital waiting for a heart transplant. He died in September.

My dad had a bad heart, but he was almost 82 when he died. At that time, Brad didn't know if he would ever agree to a heart transplant. By the end of the summer, he finally agreed and was put at the very top of the transplant list. That's how bad he was. But there wasn't enough time. A heart just didn't become available.

It was a shock when Brad died. None of us had really been sick except for Brad. We always thought, "Brad can do this." In my family there's an attitude that you can just do things. The question was how long he would last after the transplant. None of us considered the possibility that he wouldn't make it to the transplant. Even Brad assumed he'd get it. One of his sons lives in Colorado. He doesn't have a lot of money, but he was going to come and see his dad. Brad said, "Don't come until after the operation. I'm seeing everyone now. I'd like to see you then." I doubt Brad would have said that if he thought he didn't have a chance to live through it.

Our attitude was it's going to be a tough operation. A lot of people don't live very long afterwards. But that he wouldn't make it to the operation hadn't really entered our minds. He actually died about 10 days after I went to visit him. He was doing fine. Obviously weak, but he was doing fine. Then a sister from South Dakota came the next weekend. He started blacking out. He had 3 or 4 days of episodes like that; then they just couldn't revive him. My husband finally said, "I don't know why you guys were so surprised. He was really sick. You act like he was healthy and just dropped dead. But he didn't." I guess that's how it hit us at the time.

Someone said to me that when the first sibling dies, it really hits you differently than the others. I don't know. Fortunately I haven't had to go through it again, but I know at some point I will. We're basically a healthy family. Although my one grandfather died at 60, my parents and other grandparents lived into their 80s or 90s. It had been decades between the death of my last grandmother and my parents' deaths. We're not a family that deals with death very much. That was probably part of the denial of "we can do this. We're basically healthy. Brad has a bad heart, but he's healthy."

I'd say relationships in the family changed more with the death of our parents than with Brad's. When my mother died, she was the last of that generation. It makes you feel sort of like an orphan. It also makes you feel very vulnerable. To have Brad pass on five months later added to that. As long as you have a parent living, you have an older generation. You're getting older, but you're not really getting older, kind of thing. When your last parent passes on, it hits you—we are next. We even talked about that after mom's funeral when the grandchildren pointed out, "Hey, you guys are the next in line, aren't you?" Because all but one of my siblings are older than me, it probably didn't hit me as hard. There are still a lot of older ones to go before me.

I don't know whether to say we're a close family or not. We're not always talking and visiting with each other. We're scattered. We all have our own immediate families. My siblings are grandparents now so that becomes their focal point, not their siblings. As long as my parents were alive, they were a focal point. Everybody reported in to them. Because there are thirteen of us, each of us has three or four sibs that we're closest to. We talk the most with them and messages get passed on. We all know that what we're hearing may not be accurate, so if necessary we'll go directly to the person involved to verify things. We also have a brother who is a long-distance truck driver. He takes pride in passing information along. He's not very good at keeping it accurate, but at least we get an idea of what is happening. We all know to check out what he tells us.

The year my dad died, the grandchildren pushed for us to have family reunions. Since we are scattered, the cousins didn't really know one another. They're afraid that when my generation passes on the family really won't stay connected. So we started having a reunion every other year. Not everybody makes it, but a lot my nieces and nephews plan vacations around it and make it a family trip.

I have the old family homestead, but that's not necessarily the best place for the reunion. My generation wants to sit around and talk about family stuff. Some of the older cousins will sit and listen, but their wives and children really aren't that interested. So we try to have the reunion where there are activities. It's also like mini-reunions wrapped together with a big reunion. Brad's kids and grandkids are scattered. So they'll come two or three days early and do things with their family. Since that's our main time of connecting, people really do try to make those reunions. Somebody will step forward and say "Alright, I'll be in charge of the reunion." Then they take care of setting it up. Older ones somehow make that all work.

I grew up on our family farm. We worked hard. After dinner we would play ball. No matter what your age you got to play. The older ones never acted like that was a pain. Somehow they were able to be competitive among themselves, but still involve us little kids. When we played baseball, once-in-a while we'd get on base. Or when we played football, we'd get to carry the ball. While we don't talk to each other a lot, I've never had any doubt that if I needed the shirt off somebody's back, it would be there. More than any of the other older ones Brad epitomized that. For some reason, he took it upon himself to be that extra person for the young. I don't know for all of them or just for me. I still get teased, because he had to run an errand and thought he'd be a nice big brother and take me with him. Then he got a ticket or had a minor accident. It wasn't a big deal to my dad until I blurted out how fast Brad had been going.

I was the one who took care of my parents at the end. Brad would call regularly. He would talk to them; he would talk to me about what was happening. We would have long conversations. So probably the last three years, he and I became even closer. He couldn't be here a lot, so I was his connection with my parents. He also wanted to be a support for me. I had teenagers at that point. My husband was in the military and was gone a lot. So Brad and I had a lot of conversations about family, ancestors, you name it, we talked about it. In a lot of ways Brad was one of the siblings I was closest to.

When Brad died, I lost that, but his death would have hurt a whole lot more if I had still been dealing with my parents. Since they had passed on, I didn't need his support as much. I just missed the camaraderie we had. He was very easy to talk to. He was sort of the family historian. He was old enough and interested enough to get all these stories from grandparents, great aunts and uncles. The problem was he knew it all, but it was on pieces of paper in a suitcase. One day he was going to organize it, but he never had the chance to. Now I have the suitcase, but there's no organization to it. Nobody's really had the time to sit down and get into that. I learned a lot about family history just from the conversations with him.

I have two pictures of me with eleven of my siblings. There's no picture with all 13 of us. Brad's in one picture, but not my younger sister Edith. Edith is in the other, but not Brad. Now I can never have a picture like that. I directed my anger about that toward Edith. It's such a waste that she held on to a grudge for so long that the two of them couldn't be in a picture together. I did get over my anger with her, but it's sad. I can look at pictures of all of my dad's family through the years. Every time they got together, there was a sense that it could be the last time; so they took pictures. At our reunions we take pictures of everybody: pictures of just my siblings, and of each family, and of the extended family. I've got all these pictures, but not one of all 13 of us.

I don't know if it's the Scotch-Irish Presbyterian or just the farmer in us that there are seasons to life. Things die and things are born and life continues. We certainly believe there's a life after death. So it's not a big tragedy. It's a loss for us, but it's not the end of the world. That's how we were raised to view death. I wasn't part of Brad's everyday world. It wasn't as though he lived next door and I'd see him every morning. I would see him once a year or so. I did have to get used to the fact that I wouldn't talk him again. Certainly Brad is missed and we talk about him when we get together. He is part of the growing-up stories my generation shares at the reunions. Now his kids and grandchildren are part of the new stories. I can see him in his sons and daughter. But when you have a reunion with 90 or 120 people, you notice he isn't there, but it's not the same as if you have three people around the table and he's not there.

Because I bought the old family homestead and moved in after my mother died, but before Brad did, it's comforting to be there. I can remember people being there. I can picture my grandmother playing there when she was a kid. I can see her sitting on the porch peeling apples, and the porch hasn't changed. There are a lot of very friendly ghosts or spirits at that house. So living there helped me a lot in dealing with Brad's death. I can picture him there when I want to visit him.

I know he was very involved in his community He was a college professor and anthropologist. He loved to work with young people. That's why he stayed with the Boy Scouts long after his kids grew up. He was very involved with the students at the college where he worked. He influenced a lot of people. The president of the student government wrote this great letter about him. I could tell from all the letters we got and from the big obituary that there is a legacy of his contributions. I did keep the letters, so I have those reminders. But again, I wasn't a part of his world.

It's the same for all of us. We're all at least a day's drive from each other. We live our own lives and share information about ourselves. But that's not the same as being in the same community where you are running into each other all the time and able to be part of what someone's doing. We focus in different spheres that overlap. When my sister-in-law died, my brother would call quite a bit. He didn't want to be a burden to his kids, so he called his siblings. It's great that we are there for each other. I could tell when he met somebody else. The phone calls dropped off as he needed us less. Once he got married again, he got back to establishing his world. We're not always in each other's world.

I see my kids picking up the same kind of things. They're very comfortable to go far away to school. Somehow this gets passed on from generation to generation. It's okay to go off and do your thing. My daughter and my son are very close even though he's in California and she's in Pittsburgh. They're not in each other's lives on a daily basis, but she'll turn to him when she wants his opinion. She's engaged so it's not like she doesn't have anyone. But there are just certain things, probably more around family than anything, where she values his opinion, and he does the same with her. That's the same pattern that they grew up with; it's part of who they are.

In a lot of ways Brad was one of the family leaders. From my perspective, the older ones were always in charge. Brad was respected. He would step forward and say this is the way things are. People could disagree, but at least he took that first step, like the situation of my husband and me buying the farm. The farm has been in the family since the 1700s. When my mother passed on we realized what it was really worth. We couldn't afford the appraised price, but we said, "We're willing to buy it, to keep it in the family. This is what we can afford. It's not the appraised price, but we wouldn't have to pay realtors' fees. If you'd rather put it on the market, that's fine, no hard feelings." Later, I gathered that Brad made sure that everybody agreed that it was okay for us to buy the farm. He felt we offered a fair price. Maybe they could have gotten a little bit more, but if you get another $5000 and split it among 12 people, you don't get much. To him it was more important that it stay in the family. I think that's where his loss is felt. He was the one stepping forward, saying this is the way it will be. Not that he wouldn't change his mind, but at least he took a stand and people had to discuss it and agree or disagree and do something. But he pretty much had thought things through enough that people would say "Okay, that sounds good." I think his death hit the older ones more than us younger ones. They actually grew up with him and had all those years with him. I got closer to him in those last three years, but I always remembered him as the big brother who took care of me.

His being a family leader like that was kind of subtle, so no one has actually stepped into that role. Besides, we've already dealt with so many of the common family problems like the deaths of our parents, and the decision about the family farm. Now the main thing is figuring out what happens with the family reunion. Nobody wants to hurt anybody's feelings, so everybody kind of defers. Somewhere along the line, someone will say, "I'm kind of interested." A few years ago my brother in GA said he'd do it, but then an aunt and uncle said it was really important for them to do it. They have some health problems, but nobody really wanted to tell them, "You're too old to take that on." My thought was, "It's important to them. Let them do it. If it's a little disorganized, so what? We're a disorganized family anyway so it's not that big a deal. We can go with anything. Obviously it's really important to them, especially my aunt. And her kids would help." So there was a lot of back and forth on email, but in the end no one told them "no," and they organized the reunion. That's kind of how we do things. Someone takes charge and the others support that person.

What happened when my mother passed on is typical of how we do things. I called my sister Janine in South Dakota, because she was a stay-at-home person. Also, she's one of the sibs I'm close to. I called her and said "Mom passed on this morning." She then called four or five others, who then called others. We're all responsible for calling our own kids.

The question then became, "How do we split up the stuff?" My mother was a pack rat and had been in the house for 60 years. Plus there was stuff from other generations. It's not that everything was an antique; a lot had sentimental value. My decision was to do it the weekend of the funeral when everyone was here. Otherwise the stuff would sit for years; whoever picked something, someone else might have wanted it. I couldn't deal with that. I called Janine and said, "It will take you two days to drive here. Figure out how we divide it. But it has to be done this weekend." By the time she got here, she knew what she wanted to do. I wanted Janine to handle it because she had been working at antique sales and auctions. Everyone respected that she knew the value of things. She put a price on everything, then added it all up, and divided the total value by 13. It turned out each of us had $13,000 to "spend." One sister-in-law had a laptop, so she itemized everything and gave each of us a printed copy so we'd know the value of each item. We each had a number. When an item came up, if we were interested in it, we'd put our number in a jar. One of the grandchildren would pull a number. If your number was pulled and the item was worth say $500, then you've spent $500 of your $13,000 and the item is yours. Once everything was divided, we could swap, barter, or whatever. Only a sibling could put a number in. Janine had talked with someone who deals with estates. He said the only way to avoid fighting is to have a ground rule that the in-laws are not part of it. If my husband wanted something, if my daughter wanted something, it had to come through me. If I didn't want to listen to them, that was between us. It worked out really well. Everything was divided, and we were all still friends. That's fairly typical of how we do things. There wasn't a family leader who has to make all the decisions. We don't have a patriarch kind of thing. None of us looks to the oldest and says, "You've got to make all these decisions."

Even if someone disagrees or would have approached the situation differently, we defer to the person actually doing the work. Whatever I did with my parents was okay, because I was the one who was there. I'm really fortunate. From listening to friends who are dealing with aging parents, it seems they get into a lot of fights with their siblings. We've not done that. Our parents drilled into us that there is nothing more important than family. My dad refused to leave the farm to anybody. He refused to make it easy for anybody to buy the farm, because in his mind, that's how fights get started. There's favoritism. To him it was, "Yeah, it's an old family farm, but it's just land. It's not worth having a split in the family. If it is sold to someone else and houses go up on it, so be it." I just assumed that's the way families are, but it's not.

Growing up on a farm had a lot to do with it, too. Our life was working. My dad did the tractor; we did the other stuff. The oldest one was in charge; we worked together. We would take breaks; play a quick game of football or something. Especially in the winter when it was getting cold pruning trees, we would use an old apple as a ball. We'd take 20 or 30 minutes out; then work very hard to make up for it so Dad wouldn't know, although I suspect he did.

That had a lot to do with building a relationship between all of us, because we weren't a family that was involved in sports or school plays. For one thing, there wasn't a lot of that back then. For a second thing, we just weren't allowed to do that. I went to school; I went to church; I worked at home. That was my life. It wasn't a bad life; it was just different. We were each other's playmates. I have really good memories; that's probably why the farm is so comforting to me. Getting along was part of our upbringing. We may or may not like the in-laws. We may think something's a little strange, but there's an acceptance. If it works for them, that's fine. I have a brother, for example, who is a fundamentalist preacher. He accepts that we don't agree with him, and we don't get into that. Avoidance if you will. He will never agree with us, so why get into arguments over it. It's not that we never have any dissension, but we just look at it like that's where he's at and that's fine. He accepts that we're not there with him. There are still other things where we can connect. Maybe this attitude comes from having so many people in a small house. Privacy becomes a part of your mind. You don't have a room where you can go and shut the door and shut the world out. You have to do it in your mind.

14

JANET and NADINE

Janet, a minister, is one of two children. Nadine, a year younger than Janet, died in 1998 at the age of 55 from an early on-set, Alzheimer-like dementia. I spoke with Janet four years after Nadine's death.

In 1973, at the age of 30, Nadine gave birth to her first child. The prenatal care she received was not very good. Nadine was still teaching a week before she gave birth. When I visited her a week earlier, her legs and hands were very swollen. I said, "Go to a doctor," but she said, "Oh, the swelling goes down when I go to bed." She went into toxic shock and had to have a C-section. They weren't really sure that she would live. At first the baby seemed okay, but then we realized he had brain damage. He probably didn't get enough oxygen before the C-section. He's 28 now; a really sweet person; probably about seven years old emotionally and intellectually. He graduated from high school. Nadine was a real advocate for him and for others like him and was very active in their community after his birth.

Nadine was a special education, elementary school teacher. Her first noticeable symptoms appeared early in 1992. The parents of her students noticed when she met with them to work on the children's Individualized Education Plans. They told her principal about it. It started with conductive aphasia. She could think of something, but couldn't say it. The symptoms increased until, less than a year later, she quit teaching. Then a year later, she couldn't speak any more. She quit driving before that and had to have people at home watching over her.

In 1993, Nadine enrolled in a study conducted by the National Institutes of Health (NIH) and Duke University. They followed her for three years. She would spend two weeks there in the summer where they monitored how she was proceeding. Really, how she was dying. The researchers were studying genetic factors, but they said her condition was definitely related to the birth of her son. Some stroke-like symptoms probably affected a part of her brain at that time, but the damage remained latent until the early 1990s.

By the time Nadine entered the NIH study, her son was about 20. They sent him to this wonderful, residential school run by the Presbyterian Church in Virginia. He stayed there for four years during the worst part of her illness. So that was good. In 1981, they had adopted a baby girl, who was a problem and still is. It was hard for her to watch her mother go through this, because she was having psychological problems herself. We found out later that she was bi-polar.

Nadine's husband Rick, Nadine and I went together to NIH. She knew what was happening; asked questions. How will it progress? What will I die from? They were right on the line. She really died from starvation, because she couldn't swallow any more. She, Rick, and I made all the decisions about no feeding tube. She pled with us not to change our minds, because it would be so hard to watch it happen.

Over time, Nadine didn't recognize people anymore. She began wandering; pretty classic symptoms of Alzheimer's. She became very old looking quickly; lost a lot of weight; wasn't able to function; lost control of her bowels. That was one of the last things, though. She could still let you know she had to go to the bathroom and get there in time. Long before that, she had to be fed. If anything made her mad, it was people feeding her when she wanted to do it herself. She didn't mind me dressing her unless I got the wrong outfit. She was picky about outfits matching. Once when I was with Rick and her at the beach, I'd dress her in the morning and she'd shake her head when I put the wrong top on.

The day after Christmas in 1997, we put her into a nursing home not far from her house. Nadine loved her house. She and Rick had designed and built it together. Their property was beautiful, 11 acres with a big pond. Anyway, my husband, our two daughters and I went to visit for three days at Christmas knowing that we were going to move her. Looking back, what we did was deceptive. In the early days of her illness, Nadine and her in-home caregiver had volunteered at a nursing home. We told her we were going over to visit the day after Christmas. I went upstairs and packed some of her clothes. Nadine, Rick and I went in the first car; my husband came with her son and the suitcase in the second car. The nurses were ready for us; they all knew what was happening and were wonderful. While I was unpacking her things, Nadine walked into the room. She looked kind of bewildered; she couldn't talk at all by then. I said, "Nadine, you're going to stay here for a little while." She started to cry. When we left, she just kind of howled, like an animal. That tore us up. My husband took her son out. You could hear her all over the nursing home. It was just like from her soul; it was awful.

About an hour later we had to leave for Pittsburgh. I cried the whole trip. When we got home, I called Rick. He had gone over to feed her and she was already settling down which made me feel better. Still that was the worst day, even worse than her death. We were all ready for her death, but that day was so hard, because Nadine realized what was happening.

The reason we placed her in the nursing home was that Rick was still working. With her wandering at night, he couldn't sleep. I said to him, "You've got to do it." For everybody's sanity. It was one of those hard things to do, but necessary. I've been a pastor for 31 years. So many times I would say to people, "It's going to be hard, but you've got to do this." I never knew how hard it was. I really learned a lot about caregiving. There were times I'd just get so upset with her because she couldn't understand me. I learned a lot about myself; about being human and what you have to go through because you love somebody. If I hadn't loved her, it wouldn't have hurt.

Before placing her, we had all talked. Even though the nursing home was only three miles away from her house, we would never bring her back. All the experts say don't take her back. So we knew it was the last time. After she settled in, the staff would take her out. Sometimes they would take her to this little shop where she could get ice cream. Because she couldn't talk, she never asked to go home. I think she probably would have liked to go just to see it again.

By early summer she had trouble walking and was in a wheel chair. I would go down once a month after church and stay over Sunday till Monday. Probably the last three or four times, I don't think she knew who I was. Sometimes I would mention things about our home town or friends from the past, and she would remember them.

Soon after she went into the nursing home Rick and I knew for sure that we weren't going to let them do any of the things she didn't want, like the feeding tube. We talked a lot and very openly. I would say to Rick, "I think we just have to let her go." We were both ready to say good-bye. We kind of did it together. From about February through August, every time I would go down, I would really say good-bye, not knowing whether I'd see her again before she died. As it happened, we were on vacation at Rehoboth. We had stopped on Sunday on the way down; she was not doing well; she had a fever. Together we chose not to send her to the hospital. My husband and I went on to Rehoboth, about 2 ½ hours away. On Wednesday, Rick called and said, "You'd better come." She lived through the night we got there and into the next day. She died during the annual picnic at the nursing home. We said, "This is the way she would have wanted to go." They had just brought in these huge plates of food for all of us who were keeping watch.

We had the service on Sunday. The funeral was very positive. Rick was an evangelical Baptist, and she had joined that church. My cousins came; a lot of people came. People came from my church in Pittsburgh to Virginia where she was buried. After the funeral, I went back to Rehoboth, which was very tender. For almost 30 years, our families had spent so much time together at Rehoboth. The sea is very healing for me. I was so glad I could go back that Sunday and spend another week.

I'm not sure whether Nadine tried to say good-bye to me, certainly not in the last few years. I went to visit one time shortly after Rick had arranged for an in-home care-giver. They kept the screen door locked so she wouldn't wander. As I was leaving, Nadine walked to the car with me while the care-giver watched from the door. I gave her a hug and started to get into the car. The nurse called, "Come on, Nadine. Come on inside." Nadine kind of gave me this look, and I said, "It's okay, Nadine. You can go inside." She gave me another hug and started to cry. I think then she was trying to say good-bye, because she knew it was coming pretty fast. Toward the end it came faster. I had done a lot of research on Alzheimer's, and they say the faster it comes on, the faster it progresses. In some ways, seven years seemed like a short time, especially compared to a lot of other people. On certain days, it sure felt like a hell of a long time. We'd wonder when it would ever end for her and for us.

I've thought a lot about the nature of our relationship, being the older sister. I did much better at school than she did. As we were growing up, I thought of myself, not as better, but wiser. She passed me up in height in junior high. I was probably jealous of that. We were both popular, but I was more popular in general as far as offices in school and church. When I went off to college, she kind of blossomed. During the time I was in college, we weren't really all that close, because we didn't see each other very often. She'd come down to spend weekends now and then, but it wasn't like we were close. Then I went straight to seminary; then got married; then spent two and a half years in Germany.

My parents moved near my sister when they got older. She was their primary care giver while they were sick and dying. There were a couple testy times when she felt I wasn't doing enough. Working on weekends, it was tough to get away. I would have to leave on Sunday and come back Tuesday. But those trips were few and far between. Because we both are blessed with husbands, and both our jobs paid well, finances were not all that big a deal. We could help our parents who did need financial help.

We really didn't become close until we both had kids. I had my first child about five months after her son was born. So we both were pregnant together for a little while. We became very close then. Our husbands were close, still are. Her son is named for my husband who sat with Nadine all night the first night, hoping she would live through it. So they named their son after him. From that time on we were really close.

For a decade, our lives had revolved around our parents being sick and dying. After they died, we wanted to keep our closeness, our friendship. So we made sure we spent vacation time together. Sometimes the two of us would meet in Berkeley Springs for a night. One time at Berkeley Springs she got a facial and pedicure. The lady came out afterwards and asked, "Is your sister ill?" I said, "I don't think so." Then she said, "Well, I'm getting a kind of strange feeling. You know there are certain toes that are connected to parts of the body and I'm getting some strange thing with the brain."

I didn't tell this to Nadine, but that night during dinner I asked her how she was feeling; how are things going. She said, "You know, I'm wondering if something's happening because of Stevie's birth." So she sensed something coming. That was about a year before the school principal called Rick. That was the first public thing.

Nadine held on to aspects of her personality that were strong to begin with like her sense of hospitality. She loved entertaining. Even toward the end when people came to visit, as long as she knew who they were, she'd love that. She also held on to a sense of family. She had a picture and when she couldn't talk, she'd point to someone, and I would tell her about the person. She could perceive better for a longer time than she could speak. As long as we could communicate, she was always appreciative. She was a very giving person. She loved to give presents, and even when she couldn't choose things, she would make sure that my daughters, my husband, and I got gifts. She was just really very easy to be with in her illness. One week I was taking care of Nadine by myself. She became overtly angry and struck out at me. I knew it was anger at the disease. I gave her anxiety medication and she quieted down. That was probably the worst week in my life. I did participate in an Alzheimer's support group that happened to meet here at my church. They showed a movie called *She Can't Say Hello and I Can't Say Good-bye.* That was really it. There came a time when we just had to let her go.

As a person of faith, I believe that the body and mind can be ill, but the soul doesn't become ill. Toward the end, I just talked to her soul. That helped me. Even when she would be looking right at me and not responding or understanding, I could still talk to what I sensed was her soul. I did that to the end. As a Protestant, my prayers are through Christ to God, so I don't pray through saints or I don't pray for Nadine's salvation, because my faith is that she is not in purgatory having to move up. I certainly do still think, "Now Nadine, what would you want me to do about this?" Like when her daughter married with only a week's notice and I couldn't get there. I found myself thinking, "Nadine, I'm sorry I can't do this. But I just can't do it." Just thinking that, but not expecting to hear anything.

Her witness to her own illness was so strong. That taught me a lot, and I rely on that in my own work. She knew she was ill and what was coming. When we'd drive home from NIH, Rick would often drive by himself, because he was so overwhelmed. Nadine would ride with me. Toward the end, the NIH people would talk to Rick and me alone. We asked some really hard questions, and we didn't always want to share the answers with Nadine. Then I'd get in the car and she'd say, "Well, how long do they think I'll live? When will I not be able to cook or dress myself?" I decided to be as blunt as I could. I know too many pastors when somebody says, "I think I'm going to die," they'll say, "Oh no, no, no. You're going to be fine. You're going to get better." If all the indicators point to their not getting better, as a pastor I can say, "Well, someday that is going to happen, and it may be sooner than later. Do you want to talk about it?" Many people do. I talk more with people now about, not just their fear of dying, but their preparation. They want to prepare. Here at the church, we do a course about every three years called, "Where there's a will there's a way." We bring in a legal person for the real will. We bring in a medical person for a medical advanced directive. We have what's called a spiritual will, where people write down what they want and don't want for their funeral—the scriptures and hymns, etc. We share that with families. We want people to think about these things before a crisis sets in and people start denying. That's helped me a lot; to walk with people through that journey. I find more and more people are not afraid of dying. They want help doing it. If you can get your mind around the fact that you're helping this person on this journey of death, then it's a little easier not to say, "Oh, no, no, no, you're going to be fine. We're going to pray about it. God's going to heal you." That may well happen, but it may not.

This process lets people know we're willing to talk about it during the hard times, because we talked about it during the good times. I just had a lady in my office a few days ago. Her husband was diagnosed with a cancer that is not going to get better. She wanted to talk about what happens when he dies. Who does she call? What funeral home should she use? Where will the service be? What do we do about catering? She's thinking about all the details now, because she said, "I'm not going to be able to think about those things then." We have so many members here whose kids live far away, and they want to come and get their two cents in. She said, "I want to make these decisions and tell them this is the way I want it to be." We get a lot of controversy around funerals. People fly in and have to deal with their own grief and everybody else's.

I do things to keep Nadine's memory alive. Both she and Rick served as president of the board of a special education organization. There's a run/walk once a year where she is honored. I have a big collage of family photos on the wall at home. It's been there for 30 years. I still keep all the same pictures of her there. She gave me a lot of gifts, and I keep them. I'm not going to ever give those away. Nadine is buried in Virginia. Every time I visit Rick, I go to the cemetery by myself. I reminisce. I pray. I thank God for who she was, who she was to me. Sometimes I weep; sometimes I don't. I take a little flower sometimes. Sometimes I don't stay for more than five minutes; other times I just sit, remembering things we enjoyed together. I pray for her kids, because they're going to be a problem forever.

My parents donated their bodies to the University of Virginia so we have no tangible remains; didn't even get one ash back. That doesn't bother me too much. But I have to admit it's nice to be able to go and see a little headstone and see her name. It's comforting. Although I want to be cremated, there still could be some place where people could come if they want to. The cemetery here in town is gorgeous. My husband and I might buy plots there. Even though our kids aren't around, it's close to the airport if they ever want to come.

People will ask me, "As a pastor, do you think it helps to view the dead body?" I have strong feelings about children going to funerals and funeral homes. I think the earlier you do that, the healthier you are about living and dying. Those who were never allowed to go are the ones who carry around baggage. As far as wanting to see the person dead, it really depends on the person. In general, I think it's better to be there when the person dies. I knew when my dad died I wouldn't get there in time, and I didn't. So I had to resolve that. It's pretty common now to have a closed casket for visitation, but they'll allow the family to see the person. I think that makes things a lot easier for the family and for the visitors.

I had wonderful friends and support, here at the church, especially. The people I work with. My kids were very supportive, even though they were pretty young when all of this started. And my faith. I truly believe in resurrection. Nadine was a person of faith. I also believe that when Jesus said he came to give us life and give it abundantly, he meant here, not in heaven. We should be striving to work for a better life here for people. I never really gave up hope along the way. When Duke got involved, I thought, "Oh, if it's genetic, then maybe there is something we can do to stop it." That didn't work. She was involved in lots of programs. I kept putting hope in those, because some day that will work for somebody. If I had one disappointment with Rick, it was when we first went to NIH. They asked us to allow a brain autopsy, because that's the only way they can really determine if it's Alzheimer's. We both agreed, but then when she was dying, Rick said, "I've decided not to allow it." It was such a tender time; I decided not to push it. Now I kind of wish that I knew. My doctors were concerned that my daughters and I were at risk. The autopsy might have shown that one way or another.

Nadine's illness probably made me investigate my faith. Growing up in the church, then going to a Christian college, then going straight on to the seminary and right into the ministry, my faith was not tested. I've never believed theologically that God punishes people with illness. We may have lifestyles that cause illness—smoking, drinking, whatever. There are times when illness comes on because of what we've done but I don't believe God uses illness as a punishment; I'm not even sure God does it to "test people." The God I believe in is more loving; a God who grieves with us, because along the way we've chosen not to obey. When we grieve, God grieves with us. So there weren't really any times when I said to God, "Why are you making this happen?" There were times I said, "I wish it were happening to me instead of her." I would certainly say that if something happened to my kids. As far as my faith goes, I had to rethink and affirm it; affirm the things I had believed intellectually. I suddenly believed spiritually, because of watching the strength that she had in her faith, the strength Rick had and still has, the strength my family and friends brought. I know that we live and we die. Some of us die more painfully than others. Some of us live more painfully than others, too. St. Paul has a great line that whether we live or we die, we are the Lord's. I think it's the basis I had before and still do.

Some people think God has let them down. Or the God that they were brought up with isn't panning out in their adulthood because of the evil that's all around us. That's why they aren't in pews on Sunday. I wish I had an easy answer for that, but I don't. There are certain things I don't understand and never will on this side of life. There is evil and often things happen because of evil. I don't see illness as one of those. In the story of Job who lost so much, he kept asking, "Why, why, why?" I've said to parishioners, "We can ask 'why' until we're blue in the face, and we're not gong to get an answer that's good. The only appropriate question is 'how.' How do we get through this?" If you keep asking why all the time, you're not going to get an answer to the question, "Why do bad things happen to good people?" You're just not going to get an answer that is good for you. I try to help myself and my parishioners to look at all the why's until they've run out of why's. Then I try to change it so they can function, because when you're asking why all the time, you can't function as well.

When people ask, "why," they sense a loss of power. They don't have power over the health of a loved one or their own health. There has to be some realization that death is inevitable. Then you can ask "how," or "what can I do," or "how can I help this person and help myself to go through this inevitability?" You have some power, because you have to make decisions. Am I going to visit more; am I going to visit less? Am I going to force a discussion about it or am I not? Whatever it is, you have a sense of power. That's always been helpful to me. It's hard to say how we will address our own dying if we know it's coming. I do think that when people have exercised a level of faith in their health that does transfer to their illness. I've seen it happen too often.

Looking back at those years like high school, seminary, Germany, I had no initiative to stay in very much contact. It was as if we revolved around our parents. I wish I had been more intense then. Because I'm clergy, I have been able to say things in funeral homilies, particularly when a sibling has died, that reflect how they feel about each other. It gives me more understanding about how people feel about someone who has known them at all stages of their life. Nobody else has and now nobody else ever will. I just called a friend, because we've turned 60. She knows me from elementary school through high school, but not past that. Not really; not way a sibling does. I wrote something when Nadine died that was read at the funeral. There were several hundred people at the funeral, and I had known her longer than anybody in the room. I realized that ahead of time, so I wrote a couple of pages that were read by one of the ministers. I didn't want to do it, because I figured I'd cry. I do have some presence after 30 years of standing and talking all the time, but it is different when it's your own family. I've said to my daughters, "If and when you ever get married, don't ask me to officiate." I cry at weddings now, because I've been here so long that I've seen these young members of the congregation grow up." In a way, I wish I could have written something to her when she still had understanding. I know she knew I loved her. I wish there were things I could have said that she could have understood. I never did that. We did cards all the time, but nothing directly from me to her.

I dream about her, usually about her being healthy, about when we were younger. Even now, she's healthy in the dreams. I consider that a healthy sign that I'm not fixated on her dying even though it lasted so long. Usually if I dream of my parents, the four of us are all together when we were younger.

Nadine and I had always talked about traveling together; we both loved to travel. She had never been on a cruise, and that's something she wanted. After we had been at NIH the third time and they said there's no need to come back, her husband took her on a cruise. She could still converse a little bit then. She loved it. It was sad for me, because I thought, "We'll never be able to do this together."

Nadine died in 1998 and in the fall of 2000, Rick met Lynn, a widow whose husband had died of cancer. They were married the Saturday before Thanksgiving in 2001, and I helped to officiate at the service. I just love her. I never thought I'd have a sister-in-law. My nephew is really pleased. He says he has one mother in heaven and one mother on earth. Rick is so happy. He was so faithful to Nadine throughout her whole illness. Anyway, Rick and Lynn are traveling a lot now. I'm so glad for them, but I keep thinking that if Nadine were still alive that could be the four of us. Maybe Rick, Lynn, my husband and I will travel together someday, but not for a while; it would just be different without Nadine. I've already called Lynn, Nadine once. They were up after Christmas and we were just finishing dinner and carrying things out to the kitchen. I said, "Oh, Nadine, can you bring that out?" Then I realized what I had said. Lynn said, "Oh, I've been waiting for that to happen. I knew it would happen. It will happen again." She said she had called Rick by her first husband's name. So that happens.

I'm glad Nadine and I had over 50 years together. But I was really looking for 80 or 90. I have two great aunts who died two years apart in their 90s. They had lived together for over 20 years. I always thought it would be neat to live with Nadine as an old person; to appreciate what we'd had together when we were younger, what we didn't appreciate back then. The older we got the more we were friends, not just sisters.

Part of our liturgy every Sunday is the phrase "from generation to generation." My mother-in-law came to live with us two years ago and died a year ago last week. She was the last grandparent to go. So now we are the older generation, the one's we thought of as really old. We have two daughters and no grandchildren. This may sound corny, but I really think of this family constellation as woven together; something that can't be unwoven. The constellation is part in heaven and part on earth. The people—some are gone and some are here—but for me, it is still a constellation. I do some genealogy work for my family. That helps to give the sense that even though these people are physically dead, in the context of the family, they have so much influence. You have your mother's eyes, or you have your father's nose, or personality traits. I even look in the mirror now and then and see my mother, how I remember her at this age. I'll say something and my husband will say, "You sound like your mother." I looked in the mirror the other day and smiled for some reason, and thought, "I have Nadine's smile." Things about you are woven into you like a plaid that can never be pulled apart whether you're living or dying. The generations continue on down. I don't think of myself as alone or lonely. At times I wish that I could pick up the phone and call Nadine, particularly when difficult things happen within the family. I wish I could lean on her in the way you lean on family, instead of friends. Still, I sense the constellation; some of it is behind the sun; some of it is in front of the sun; some of it's eclipsed; some of it isn't. But the family constellation is still there.

I sense I didn't deal with guilt as much as I should have, with myself or with others. I told a story in a sermon on May Day that just blew people out of the water. One May Day when I was about 5 and Nadine was 4, we lived in a place where there were thousands of violets. Nadine went out and picked this whole big bunch of them and brought them into the kitchen for mother. Then she went to the bathroom and I came in and picked them up and gave them to my mother. People just couldn't believe that this nice lady preacher could do that. I wanted to let people know that we all do things like that. I forget the rest of the sermon, but I'm sure that story is all they'll remember. Things like that are in the backs of our minds, in our memories. The guilt or shame or whatever it is that we need to deal with. I sense that a lot grief about siblings comes from stuff that happened decades ago. Often it is little things like the violets, that aren't resolved.

There can also be resentment, maybe even more than grief. Usually it's over what the siblings did or didn't do when the parents were dying; the care that was given or not given. Or it may be over financial aid that parents gave one sibling more than another; or one got a better education than another. I see that between living siblings when the parents die. A woman about a month ago said, "I don't think I'll ever forgive my parents because they allowed my brother to go to college and told me I couldn't." I mean this woman was 65 or 70 and was still angry, even though she probably could have gone to college later on her own. She married a wealthy man and has done a lot of good in the community, but she still harbors that resentment. I wondered, "How are you and your brother going to relate if this is the one thing you happen to mention to me." We were out here having coffee after the service talking and this came up, out of the blue. I said, "If you want to come in and talk, please do." She hasn't, but that doesn't mean she never will. Those kinds of things people do harbor.

Maybe it's some sort of Freudian competition for parental love. Then when the parents are gone, where does that competition go? Fortunately, this didn't happen with Nadine and me, because we were pretty equal as far as class and education and living style. But competition can transfer to something else like how your children do. My kids were really smart; both were high school valedictorians. Then there's my nephew who's brain damaged and my niece who hasn't finished high school. If Nadine were alive and well, she wouldn't say this to me, but I'm sure that she would think, "Why did your daughters do so well and my children didn't?" Every so often I sense that in Rick, but he's been wonderful to my kids. It's almost as if he's substituting them for his. I sense sibling competition can transfer from one generation to another. I see that all around here, because some people tend be showy about their money, or their wealth, or their jobs, or their education, or whatever. There's a strong sense of competition among the kids at the local high schools. We have to watch out for that in how we program things at church. You have to deal with those feelings some time, whether it is before the person dies or after. It has to be dealt with, or it's going to be transferred to the next generation. That's unhealthy for everybody. The reason I use examples like the violets when I preach is to make people think about the petty things that we remember, that we have to get past. There's more to life than this.

15

RACHEL and BRIAN

Rachel is the youngest of four siblings. Her brother, Brian, was 44 when he died following surgery to remove several brain tumors. Rachel was about 35 at the time of Brian's death, which had occurred 30 years before Rachel and I talked. Both of Rachel's parents were living at the time of Brian's death. Her father was a minister and so the family was conversant with death and funerals. Brian was married and had two young sons. His widow, Lottie, never remarried. Rachel and she are close friends, and she continues to participate as a member of Rachel's family.

Brian was on sabbatical from his high school teaching job and was living in England. In January of that year, he blacked out and couldn't drive any more. He was very frightened when he had to go to the doctor in London for all kinds of tests. They didn't discover anything significant. Back in 1969, you didn't call people in Europe. We received letters in which he complained about not driving. But he, his wife and two young sons went on with their plan to visit his wife's family in Germany.

They returned to the United States in July. I'm not sure why, but he went again to the doctors and the neurologist sent him to a neurosurgeon. He had surgery in the middle of August from which he did not recover. This may be a memory that has absolutely no ground in fact, but he kept singing, "The strength is o'er the battle done." We sang that at his funeral. I don't know how straightforward he felt the doctors in England had been with him. I don't know if he was scared out of his wits. But I think he knew he was a goner as early as January.

In 1968, my mother had been diagnosed with cancer. I went with her for her one month, two month, three month check ups. The summer Brian came back to the States, my nine-year-old son Frank was hit by a car and had a fractured skull and a fractured leg. So I didn't see Brian but talked to him on the phone. He called the day that Frank was hit by the car to say how worried they were. All of this was going on at the same time. My house became the place where people called to leave messages and to drop off kids since I had to be home with Frank anyway.

The day Brian went for surgery, my mother had an appointment at the same hospital, and I was with her. Before his surgery, they asked, "Do you want to go in to see him?" I said, "No. I'm not up to it." I was still strung out from Frank. I remember very clearly saying, "No, I couldn't." My parents were there. Whether I didn't want to fall apart in front of them, I don't know. Lottie was there, too, and I just said "no" because I was not up to it.

The surgery was much more complex than they expected. There were several different kinds of tumors in several different places. The day after Brian's surgery I took Frank to the doctor to have his cast checked. I said, "We're not in terrific shape, because Brian had brain surgery yesterday." The doctor looked at me and said, "They were in the next operating room and things were not going well."

I got a couple of phone calls from the hospital. One was, "the wound is swelling." I remember praying that he would die. It was my understanding that he would have been impaired if he had survived. He would have been very unhappy if he were unable to care for himself physically or not be able to finish a sentence. There was a swelling in the brain and I prayed that the swelling would continue—would kill him. Then the phone call came that he had died. I remember getting out of bed in the middle of the night because I couldn't sleep. I had a terrible stomach ache. I wrote to the people next door, who were away, to say, "Brian just died." I did have second thoughts about praying that he would die. I pondered that after the fact. I would do that again, however. Both pray and ponder.

I didn't see him in the casket. It was closed because they couldn't clean up all the effects of surgery. So there was no good-bye although I don't think I was up to it. For what reason, I'm not sure. At the funeral my mother was standing outside of the little country church and saying, "Well, I don't want to go in, but I don't want to stand out here any longer either." I remember walking to the graveyard that was just behind the church. Lottie was being escorted by the funeral director, and I said to myself, "This is tacky." So my husband and I went up and walked with her. You don't walk with strangers to the grave. I feel very strongly about that.

We were a tight-knit family. We all left home and then all came back, which was okay. My oldest brother got married and had six children before any of the rest of us got married. I'd say we always got along pretty well although we didn't all come home for Sunday dinner. Brian had a wonderful mind. He would do *The New York Times* crossword puzzles in ballpoint pen and got very annoyed when he couldn't do them anymore. That was VERY frustrating to him. He was a very verbal, smart-ass type. Loads of fun. Very social. At one time he had been in a gay relationship and this was something you didn't talk about back then. So Brian was always a difficulty in some ways. He met Lottie. She knew what was going on in Brian's life; they married and had two boys who were 6 and 4 when Brian died. Brian was difficult to live with. I remember that there was an endocrinologist at the hospital who lived around the corner from us. She asked how my sister-in-law was doing, and I remember saying, "If Lottie could live with Brian alive, Lottie can certainly live with him dead." And she has. She's done very well. She's a very close member of the family. I didn't have sisters, so I've got to have sisters-in-law. We're still very close.

After Brian died, my mother gave me some money to have a massage, which was wonderful. I had been crawling up the walls, out of my head, because of the thing with Frank. I had my out of town nieces and nephews staying at the house. So she said, "You need some care." That was wonderful. That was something my mother did for me. But I had this long-lasting awareness that she and my father had been wounded in a way you hope you never are. One of the young men in the congregation where my father was a visiting pastor had lost his sister. He told me, "Your dad comes to visit my folks and they talk about how tough it is to lose a child." I think my parents started to age or went over a certain hump. Dad was 70 and mother was 69.

It must have been terrible to have a child die, because it goes against the grain of time. But also, I didn't want my parents not to face it. You know, this is what life is, to hurt sometimes. So don't gloss it over or not talk about it. We did talk about things pretty well with the exception of homosexuality.

My dad was a minister, and he had buried people of Brian's age before. It was hard for him and my mother to not be professional, to be cared for. We just had to say, "Be quiet, Dad. You're his dad. Just roll with it." That was a tough thing. To see them have to deal with it. More so than me.

My parents worried a lot about Lottie; how she was going to cope with two kids. They kind of hovered over her. She did not move back to California, because she knew she'd always be just her parents' daughter if she did. She wanted to stay who she was. So she went back to teaching school. Brian was buried in August, and Lottie went back to teaching after Labor Day.

I think that Brian's actual death hurt so much, that I was numb. I got physically sick. Several months after Brian's death my oldest brother developed diabetes; the brother closest to me had a heart attack; I got ulcers. I lost weight. It was the only time in my life when it hurt to sit on a hard chair. But you get by with help from friends. Then somehow the numbness goes away. Maybe you steep in the support of friends so that hard lump softens. Over time, oxidation lessens the soreness of it. If you keep it out on the shelf, it's going to dry up; it's not going to fester.

The first Christmas, my husband, kids, my parents, a neighbor and I celebrated Christmas at Brian and Lottie's house. Lottie and the boys were at her parents in California. That was a tough year. We were bursting into tears at dinner.

The following August, I was waiting for some disaster. Also when I got to be 44, I wondered, "Am I going to make it through this year?" I've always been aware of anniversaries. I used to get hyper at my kids' birthdays; maybe it was my body remembering the hard work it did. I remember 44 was tough and then that first year. The first August.

Lottie wanted to be away from home during the time Brian had been in the hospital. So she and I rented a fishing camp that was run by a woman who had been my oldest brother's baby sitter. I didn't drive so my parents drove and then they decided to stay in another cottage. That griped Lottie and me, because we wanted to be alone. I said something to my dad, and he said, "Well, I thought you needed a man around the place." What they really wanted was to be there, too.

Three years after Brian died, my other brother had a valve in his heart replaced. He had been monitoring his health after Brian died. I remember going through the same, "What might happen?" Again it was friends who helped. A friend who had had heart surgery took all of us under his wing. Even now—one of my surviving brothers has had a quintuple by-pass and the other has had surgery for an aortic aneurysm—so I begin to think, "Who's going to be left on the ball field?" I think it's important to remember that we were pains in the neck to each other. Brian and I would fight more than my other brothers, but maybe he would fight with the other brothers, too.

There are little remembrances. Like around Christmas, or Easter, or birthdays, people reminisce. My husband's father was quite palsied for a while. We lived in a house that had a clerestory window and beyond that was a florist's greenhouse. If dad wanted to drink his cereal out of the bowl, he would tell the kids, "Look at the birds on the greenhouse." So whenever we want to do something like that at the table, we just say, "Look at the birds on the greenhouse." I'm sure most families have things like that.

At my 50th high school reunion, I saw some people who didn't know Brian had died. They remembered the Christmas dance during the senior year in high school. Tartan jackets for men had just become popular. Brian showed up all the guys who had worn tartan jackets, because he had studied in Scotland and had a real kilt that he wore to the dance.

My mother died at age 93. At the reception after the memorial service, a man came up to me. I hadn't seen him since I was a kid when we spent our summers at a vacation home next to his. I said, "Those two young men over there are Brian's boys. Go over and talk to them." He had a really good conversation with them, they told me later. It was nice to be able to do that, to connect the generations that way. The world keeps going around and every now and then you get a surprise. It was as though someone was splicing something from way back into the present.

My dad had a Guernsey mug which is a silver pot that you put hot water in when you are making tea. I had inherited it. When Brian's son got his Ph.D., I handed on the Guernsey mug with a note that said, "This was originally for hot water but your father always said that it would be terrific for a martini." It was nice to be able to pass on that memory. At certain stages in the kids' lives we'd think, "Wouldn't it be nice if Brian were around?" But he was a cantankerous person in some ways. A lot of life was easier without him. Every now and then my husband and I wonder what kind of old man Brian would have been.

From one point of view, I'd say we cut our teeth on Brian's death. The first one paves the way. Between Brian's death and the death of my other sister-in-law, my father died, my mother-in-law died, my father-in-law died, my mother died, in that order. When my dad died, we were pretty wishy-washy. We knew the surgeon pretty well and he could have said, "This is it, kids." But he didn't say that, so there was not the up-frontness. I don't know whether it was as medically confused as it was emotionally, but we didn't deal with it directly. My mother died in a nursing home, having been out of it for about three years. I remember saying goodbye, but there wasn't a heck of a lot to say goodbye to. I was also mealy-mouthed then. It would probably have been better if I had said, "This is probably it, Mom, and I'm going on a trip."

My sister-in-law was 63 when she died. She was diagnosed with colon cancer at New Year's and was given six months to live. She said that was the worst thing a doctor could have told her. Don't give them a timeline. Nevertheless, in that time, her daughters took her back to Slovakia so she could see the town her mother and father grew up in. That was terrific. They came to see us. The daughter was engaged to a very nice man, and he came to visit her. Then when she finally took a turn for the worse, she had a hospital bed in the dining room. We'd say grace and hold hands with her while she was in bed. The people next door sent over meals. People just took care. People were there all the time. Her daughters took turns flying in every other weekend to be with her and their dad. I was extremely impressed with how these daughters were physically able to care for their mother. They had hospice. Nobody was kidding anybody about anything.

Lottie and I drove up to see her about 10 days before she died. My brother met us at the door and said, "We just want you to know she looks terrible." She did. We said good-byes. When she died they had an open casket. My brother said, "This is what death looks like." However, my sister-in-law's ashes have not been buried yet. I have no idea what that's about. She collected hats, so we were all going to wear hats. So far this hasn't happened. The up-frontness of my sister-in-law's death was very helpful to all of us.

At one point we moved to New York because my husband took a job there. The minister's wife was dying of cancer, and we became very good friends. She had other friends that I also became friends with. One of these friends said, "Rachel, you've got to have a pact with me. If we know the other one is dying, we've got to talk about it." My friend got a cold, and I was wondering if I should say, "Just because you're dying of cancer, doesn't mean you can't get a cold." She was very direct and we would talk about strength and things like that. My other friend and I would say, "When do you have the heart-to-heart conversation?"

We had a friend who is a nurse and she had gone to help care for my sister-in-law. At that point, they needed people around the clock to care for her. The nurse said, "Can you let go? What are you waiting for?" My sister-in-law said, "Not yet." But within about an hour, she died. It's like the first funeral I had as a Pastor. I visited my parishioner in the hospital and his breathing was very labored. I told him it would be okay for him to die; we'd take care of his wife. He died in about 35 minutes.

It can be very different between a sudden death and a longer one. One man I know, got sick Wednesday morning and went to the doctor, came home and, as my mother would say, woke up dead Thursday morning. His colleague had had cancer for six years. Their memorial services were so different. They were different people, but also the preparation in each case was so different.

Brian's death did not shake my faith. There's always stuff I've considered dirty pool that God plays. There's a wonderful line from St. Teresa, "If this is the way you treat your friends, no wonder you have so few of them." For the most part I don't have regrets, except for the homosexuality issue. If it had been a different time, we might have talked and that would have been better. But it was the nature of the time. Still his life might have taken a whole different course. There might not have been sons. So no, I don't have a list of "I wish I had." I'm just delighted to have Lottie. She's a neat person and the kids have turned out very well.

16

MARTA and HETTIE

Marta is a friend who had first expressed some misgivings about talking with me. She felt I wouldn't be interested in her story because she hadn't been close to her sister. When I explained that was not the case, she agreed to the interview. Her relationship with her sister turned out to be more complex than Marta's initial comment had indicated.

Marta is the youngest of five siblings. She is about 13 years younger than a first-born brother; 7 years younger than Hettie, the sister who died; 5 years younger than the next sister; and 4 years younger than the next to youngest sister.

Hettie died in a paupers' hospital in Texas of complications of alcoholism, probably cirrhosis of the liver. I can't remember how long she was in the hospital, maybe a week. Maybe it took her a week to die. She was 44, I think. I haven't been to the cemetery for a while. When I walk past her tombstone, I usually am reminded of her age, either 44 or 46. I would have been 39, 40, somewhere around there. My mother and another sister flew to Texas and were with her the entire time. Her daughter was also there for part of the time and her second husband. She had told my mother that she wasn't drinking anymore; but when they went to Texas, she said she never went a day without drinking.

I was talking with my counselor about her drinking and death. I was thinking that I'd better start turning this over a little bit so I could make sense of it. We were talking in generalities and she asked, "What are you feeling in your body now? Where do you notice sensation in your body?"

I said, "In my jaw and in my back. Why?"

She asked, "Can you figure out what that is?"

"I am really very conflicted about whether or not I want to talk with you about this."

She asked, "Well, what do you think about that?"

I said, "It's in the back of my jaw. It's something I don't want to talk about."

Then she said, "Yeah. Probably. What about your back?"

I said, "I have no idea. No, I can't figure out why in my back. Usually when I get tense, I feel it in my neck, not there."

She said, "I'm finding this interesting because it's near your spine. Weren't you saying that even though you know alcoholism is a disease, you always thought that you just need to be strong enough to overcome it?"

Her read was that I was troubled by the lack of spine, no backbone. That really blew me away. I like that she went to the somatic awareness. It was easy to do the jaw part, but the back part threw me. We had been talking about my relationship to Hettie. Of all my siblings, she was the one I admired the most. She was the only sibling I was ever close to in any way. She was the sibling I'd visit.

Hettie lived in a town near the college I attended, so I'd stop by on my way to or from school. I always admired her. She was very, very bright; very capable; a wonderful musician like our grandmother who was a pianist and a music teacher. Our grandmother lived upstairs from us. She was extremely frail the whole time I was growing up. It was remarkable to me how she played the piano because she had such power in her hands. She looked like the slightest little breeze would knock her over, but something came through in the piano playing, and my sister reminded me of that power.

When I was in college I'd drink, but Hettie never did. She didn't like the taste of alcohol. When she did start drinking, it was really sweet wine. I'm not sure why she started. It was gradual; she started with the wine, but it wasn't out of control. She always seemed content with her suburban housewife life. She wanted to have a zillion kids. She loved children and seemed very happy. We'd have Christmas at her house when the kids were very young. When she started drinking, my response to it was "look at what you've done to me; you've disappointed ME." So the tightness in the jaw was more than an unwillingness to talk. I'm still mad at her for drinking and not shaping up. I know I am.

A constellation of things may have started her drinking. After her first child, she had several miscarriages; then a girl, then several more miscarriages. She and her husband adopted a boy. Soon after the adoption, she got pregnant, went full term, and had a boy. So she had three boys under five. Her husband was very content to have his boys, his house, the Pirates on the radio or TV, and an Iron City Beer. To him that was life. I think Hettie became discontented; she needed more intellectual stimulation. Her husband didn't want her to work which was a big battle. Her marriage was going sour. She was a city person; living out in a small town was too isolating for her. She was very social, very gregarious. Then there was a friendship with a priest. They were very, very close. I never knew the exact nature of that relationship although I can speculate now what it might have been. He committed suicide. All this was developing over five or six years. Eventually she left her husband and she, the three boys and her daughter moved in with my parents and me. She was a nurse, so she got nursing jobs. She was drinking pretty heavily by then, but never enough to interfere with her work. They lived with us for about two years and then moved up the street.

Then her house burned down. She was having a lot of financial problems, and her furnace was shut off because she hadn't paid her bills. She was using a space heater which caused a fire. Her house and the one next door burned down. Her husband took the boys back. Her daughter was 18 by then, so she stayed with Hettie. At some point her daughter got a job in Texas, and Hettie moved there. That's where she met her second husband.

For a while no one perceived she had a drinking problem. Then she started drinking whiskey and my mother began to realize there was a problem. Mom tried to talk her into getting help. By the time she moved in with us, it was pretty bad. We saw it progressing. On occasion, my mother and I would talk about it, but I never talked directly to Hettie about it. I don't think I was capable of doing that. I tend to internalize and repress. I call myself the Queen of Repression. There's no problem so big or complicated that it can't be run away from. That's what I do best; I run away from them. I didn't try to stop her drinking.

I guess my attitude was, "Come on. Decide you're not going to do this anymore and stop." She had gall bladder disease and was told she couldn't drink any more or she would kill herself. And she did. I think that is literally what she wanted to do.

It was such a waste. Because I tend to internalize things and not confront them, the feelings turned to anger. I got mad at her; I'm still mad at her. I know intellectually that alcoholism is a disease, but there's some blockage with the emotional connection. My dad was also an alcoholic, a periodic alcoholic or binge drinker. As awful as that could be on occasion, he just quit for 20 years while his children were growing up. I'm really the only one who lived with him when he went back to drinking. I thought, "Dad could quit; why can't you?" It was almost as if everything was a lie—I want all these kids; I love my children—all of that. I wanted to say, "If you love your children, you wouldn't act this way." I can say over and over again, "It's the disease not the person," but the person disappears. They're not there any more. There's something else, and it's foreign; it's not who I knew. It was easy for me to distance myself.

When she actually died, I didn't feel very much. That sounds awful, but I didn't. I felt more for my mother than for my sister. That was part of why I was mad at her, watching what she did to my mother. Thinking back, any sadness I felt, I felt through my mother. My mother is sad because she lost her daughter, and I'm sad for her. I'm not sad because this is my sister. I don't remember the funeral. It fits, doesn't it though? My sister and my mother died two years apart. I remember all about my mother's funeral. I remember lots of conflict with my sisters at Mom's funeral.

When Hettie died, one of her boys, my godson, went to the funeral home, but he just couldn't take it. He got an upset stomach during the family viewing and threw up. He went to our house, and he never went back. His brothers tried to get him to go to the funeral mass, but he wouldn't go to his mother's funeral. I remember that, but not the funeral home. I remember the three boys coming and her daughter being there.

Hettie's death didn't have an impact on my relationship with my other siblings. It didn't draw us closer. My family is not real demonstrative. There's sort of a tacit understanding that everybody loves each other, but people don't show affection. I wouldn't call it cold; it's just that emotions weren't talked about. We've never really called each other every day. My brother was almost an adult when I was a kid. He was in the service for a long time, so I don't even remember him being around very much. Nothing changed there because we hardly ever saw each other. I don't think anything changed with the other siblings.

The books on grief and mourning don't make a lot of sense to me. They say there are so many years and you should work through things. There are stages of grieving like denial and so forth. It's time to deal with the grief or it's time to be over the grief. I suppose there's a norm about that. In my own case, I don't think I ever grieved. I'm on the deferred grief plan.

I repress things I don't want to deal with. I'm very good at deferring them. Literally, I don't think about them. I have some very powerful defenses. It may be why it takes a while for things to sift in. For example, if something happens at the school where I teach, everyone is in an uproar. That's never my reaction, never. My first response is to intellectualize it. Let me think this out. Let me look at it this way and that way. Intellectualizing distances me. That's my first defense. Even when I am dealing with something, I'm never dealing on an emotional level. I'll sift through it in a cognitive way.

I used to tease about people always wanting me to talk. My friend, Kitty, always thought it was so deadly that I wouldn't talk about things. I kept insisting, "Kitty, this works fine for me." I'm not sure it always does though. Maybe it's my age saying, "It's time to get in touch with a lot of things." I don't know if that's really it.

I definitely pay a price for not talking—like the ability to conduct relationships, to have relationships. I won't say anything; I just go silent.

In emotional matters, especially if I'm hurt, I frequently won't express it; the door shuts. I just expect people to know. "What do you mean you need to know how I feel? You should just understand that." I expect them to read my mind. That can be detrimental.

I'm not sure I'm ready to think yet about regrets. I'm getting there; even doing this interview represents a turn on my part, to be willing after 13 years to address my feelings in any way. I bet I haven't mentioned this to my counselor more than two times— once a long, long time ago; then just last week. There's a line in Edgar Lee Master's *Spoon River Anthology,* "To have a thousand memories and not a single regret." That probably holds true until you're about 22. You have to live a lot to have regret. I wasn't very kind to my sister, wasn't at all forgiving, wasn't understanding. I felt for my mother and what she was going through, but that would just make me condemn Hettie all the more. I think the time has come to start turning these things over.

I cut off a lot of memories. I might get an image because I often think in images. I can't get past the image of sitting at her dining room table or her living room and talking. But there are so few images. When something is troubling me, I have dreams. They are strange, very disturbing dreams. Not scary, just unsettling. The dreams may be part of my tendency to repress feelings. That's what comes up in dreams. Consciously you may not be aware of any feelings, but unconsciously you're making connections. Then they come out in dreams that seem totally unrelated.

I haven't thought about creating any type of memorial to Hettie. My counsellor did suggest that I should try to seek a more balanced portrait. She said, "Maybe you had your sister on a pedestal when she was younger. Then when she fell off, it was like a black and white world. Can you find something that's sort of in the middle, human. Try to humanize her rather than idealize and demonize." I'm trying that, but it's only been a week, so I'm not there yet.

Drinking is such an awful thing. At first I was just shocked. I couldn't ever figure out how she could go from not even liking alcohol to the decline. There's something awfully powerful in those addictions. It's really mystifying to me. My one nephew became an addict, drugs and alcohol. Hettie's daughter almost became a mother figure. First Hettie followed her to Texas; then my nephew. She took care of him until he got so bad that she wouldn't let him in the apartment, and he lived on the streets. He eventually found his way to a monastery. He's dry now. He just stopped drinking. He was able to do what Hettie wasn't. She lost everything, but still she didn't stop drinking.

One of the things I assimilated from my mother was, "Don't be weak. Don't ever be weak." It wasn't ever spoken in those words, but she modelled it. The message came through, "No matter what happens, you just plug right along. If there's not enough of this, then you make do. If you don't have this, you just don't dwell on it." That's a line of hers that I always remember, "Marta, don't dwell on it." When I was whining and complaining and feeling sorry for myself about giving up cigarettes; she'd say, "Don't dwell on it." I was in my late 20s, but that became the exemplar for me. The overriding idea is don't be weak, be strong. Emotion is weak; you have to be strong. In my twisted psyche, that's what happened.

I started seeing a counselor about two years ago for work-related things. She said, "If that's where you want to start, that's fine; but six months down the road we'll get to what you really want to deal with." Actually doing my doctoral dissertation helped move me along; it was transforming. It was sort of a safe place to go, but it did change me. It started that process of reflecting.

I knew from the start that it would feel risky. I was studying my teaching which I'd spent 30 years doing, and I didn't take that lightly. I would have to be willing to confront whatever it was that I turned up. Given my penchant for not looking at things, I knew it wasn't going to be pleasant all the time, but it wasn't as bad as I thought.

Somewhere along the line, I had a long, dark night of the soul. I literally disappeared. Nobody could talk to me. Nobody could call me. I answered no phones. I had no communication with anyone. I was down as low as I was going to go. I said to myself, "You're either going to shape up, put one foot in front of the other and keep moving. Or you're going to make a conscious decision that this is not what you wish it to be or need it to be. But you are going to do it consciously, and you're not stepping foot into the world again until you do." I was exhausted. I felt like someone had beaten me up. I didn't sleep.

I knew I'd have to put aspects of my teaching life out on the table and name them. Like here's what I'm doing and that's "false pride." Here's something else, and I'm going to name that "fear," and ask, "What am I afraid of?" So that helped to soften me toward the process. Also I knew if I was going through this painful process, it would have to be fulfilling. If it wasn't worthwhile, who wants the pain? In the end, that's the gift in suffering through a painful process—a transformation for self-understanding.

17

NED and DERRICK

Ned is the fourth of five siblings. His older brother, Derrick, died at age 63 from cancer when Ned was 56. Ned has two older sisters, one younger sister. During the year that his brother died, Ned's father died of a heart attack and his younger sister's son contracted a rare form of cancer at age 16 and died at 18 just after graduating from high school. Ned describes his father's death as the most "normal," in a sense of being the least traumatic, because his father had had a heart attack at age 39 and had had heart problems off and on over the years. His death, while sudden, was not totally unexpected, and Ned feels his father had led a full life. His brother's and nephew's deaths were much more traumatic. Ned is now retired from law practice and suffers from Parkinson's disease.

My father was very stern and had high expectations for us. I respected him, but was also somewhat intimidated. My brother, being older, had a different, closer relationship with him. They would go hunting and fishing together. By the time I was growing up, my father was very involved with his work and didn't have as much time to spend with me. So Derrick would take me hunting squirrel, crow, and other small game. On Saturday and after school, he would take me in tow so we developed a pretty close bond. My brother was an avid hunter and particularly more of a fisherman. I share that with him. Fishing is wonderful; it's great therapy. I still love to go out in the woods. I don't really care to kill anything anymore, but to walk as much as I can with my Parkinson's.

Along with my father and me, Derrick belonged to a hunting and fishing camp up in northern Pennsylvania. We shared a lot of wonderful times there, so we scattered half of his ashes in the camp's trout stream. His widow gave the other half to me. Two years after he died, my church dedicated a columbarium that they had been building. Derrick's ashes were interred there. I was happy to do that, wanted to do that, to keep his presence close at hand. That gave me a sense of peace, some closure. We didn't live near each other, but we'd talk on the phone at least once a week. It's in a beautiful setting, and I'll go over there after church. So he is nearby.

By the time he was diagnosed, they couldn't find the source of the cancer; it was everywhere. I'll never forget seeing him; they set up a hospice bed in the dining room of his home. I was still practicing law at the time, but I'd drive down a couple of times a week. In the last week, my sisters were at his bedside. It brings tears thinking about it. He had terrible sunken eyes. He just didn't die. He wouldn't die. We'd say, "It's okay. Let go." He just hung in there. It was such a prolonged agony. It was a horrible time. The whole thing was to keep him comfortable. We all accepted that he was dying. It was for his own peace and comfort that we were hoping he would let go. It seemed like he was holding on, holding on to not dying. It was just tragic, a horrible death.

I didn't talk to him about why he wanted to hang on. I would say to him, "Derrick, you've had a wonderful life. You've done it all. They can't do anything more for you. Why don't you go to meet your Maker? Why are you resisting? You know I love you." He was a hard-nosed guy. He was very strong, always an in-charge kind of guy. Strong opinions. It was draining to watch his decline. I'd drive home, go to work, and then drive back the next night. It was very difficult.

I felt better being there. I wanted to be there. I can't tell you why. It was just over such an extended period of time. It was supposed to be quick; he was just riddled with cancer. It was such a difficult situation. We prayed to the Good Lord to take him away.

His death itself was not peaceful, not serene. With a sudden death, sometimes it's harder; it's initially shocking. You didn't expect the person to pass away. With Derrick, we knew what was happening; we watched the deterioration, slower and slower and slower. A couple of months before he died, he came up and the five of us siblings had lunch together. He had been in and out of the hospital and had different kinds of chemotherapy, went through the whole battery. He was in great pain. It was just such a horrible way to leave this world. He was such a fighter. He never complained. I continue to hold him up, still respect him. The grief is just there. You carry it with you.

Derrick wasn't a terribly religious person. He was in a church, but he was not very devout. Nor am I. Though I do have a pretty strong faith, but I keep that to myself. I hold my faith to myself and worship as I see fit, as I feel comfortable with. Derrick didn't reveal too much of himself to too many people. He had a lot of friends—business associates, hunting and fishing friends. He was well liked. But he was also very strict and had his beliefs. He did alienate some people. That disturbed me, but I did understand it. He spent a lot of time at the fishing camp. He'd use it as an entertainment venue. There were a couple of members who didn't like him, because if they did something he didn't like, he didn't hesitate to tell them. He wasn't a politician and didn't worry much about diplomacy. For example, if a guest was carrying a loaded gun where he shouldn't have, Derrick would say something and member might be upset about that. My point is that he was admired and respected. He was loved, not only by his family, but by some of the people at the camp. A group wanted to build a fishing pavilion and raised money for it. We built a beautiful pavilion where they can have barbeques and events. We placed a plaque there. Some people didn't like the idea of memorializing anybody, but I think it was more that they didn't like Derrick. He wasn't perfect. He and I would do things differently, but he had so many good qualities.

Whenever I fish, I think of my brother and the good times we had. As cornball as this may seem, I really identify with the movie, *A River Ran Through It*. I watch it frequently, because there are so many parallels to my brother and me. Even though he was considerably older than me, we had a very special relationship. He was very accomplished. For example, he was a world class trap skeet shooter. He was good at what did. He did what he wanted to do. It's a comfort to think that he lived life on his own terms, as he wanted to live it.

My sisters and I have grown closer since Derrick's death. Two live in this area. We get together. We were very supportive of each other during Derrick's illness. They were unbelievably committed to his care. We were very close and that relationship continues to this day.

I know many people may seriously question their faith when they lose a spouse or family member. My faith is pretty strong. I believe that when your time comes, your time comes. Try to live life to the fullest, get the most out of it. I have Parkinson's, and it will get progressively worse. I'm trying to slow it down. I want to do as much as I can.

It was a very difficult time with Derrick's death and the death of my father and nephew. That was terrible. I can't imagine. I have two children and three step-children. My wife and I have talked several times about losing one of your children before you die. It has to be a horrible pain. They are still very emotional. It was difficult for them, for all family members. I probably said less than other family members about it, but I thought about it all the time. I couldn't get it out of my mind; the loss of a child, a loved one. My father's death was perhaps the easiest loss, because he had had a full life. With a young person, that suffering is so hard. His parents took him to the Mayo Clinic and took him to Sloan Kettering. They tried to find a cure. You get on the Internet and try to find some hope. You chase rainbows you have no business chasing because you hope for some cure. It was such a devastating time. It did affect me and my work. It cast a pall over everything. I couldn't get it off of my mind.

Derrick's death affected my concentration. He held on for three months. He was just so skinny, nothing to him, like he walked out of a concentration camp. Early on I did hope for a cure. You have to hope. But at the end, I remember driving down and praying that by the time I got there he would have been taken.

Derrick was such a hard-nosed guy; he did not complain. He didn't talk about it, till the end. He became more and more open with me. He'd call me in and say, "Close the door." We'd just talk. He knew he was dying, but I'd let him be in charge of the conversation, because of his personality. I'd go in and we'd talk about his day; we'd talk about the weather; we'd talk about sports; we'd talk about the news, the fishing club, events, people. We could get down to the core real quick. With other people, he tried to make them feel at ease. He consciously didn't want anyone to be turned away because of the way he looked. He wanted to make other people feel comfortable. He appreciated their visiting.

I received support from my colleagues, friends, and law firm partners. The other partners knew it had to be affecting my work, but they were very understanding. My sisters and I were supportive of each other. We'd be at Derrick's house and gather in the kitchen or family room and talk. It was such a horrible death, we'd talk about praying that it would end for him.

I don't really have any special words of wisdom for others who are going through this sort of thing. You have to accept the reality of the situation. Some people question why. I don't think you can dwell on that. I try to steer the conversation toward what we're dealing with. Obviously you're trying to help the people who are most emotionally affected to feel comfortable. Try to focus on the good times, too. Not just after the person has passed away, but during the process of death. I don't know how they train the hospice people, but they were wonderful. Being realistic about what the situation is and dealing with it in a realistic manner instead of hoping. There's a time when hope is gone; you have to accept that and start to look toward the moment of death. That is a different context. You'll know when that moment comes. It's recognizable. It's not just a doctor's pronouncement, "This is it." It's a sense of acceptability that will naturally be there. When that comes, there's a relief.

The hope area is dangerous. You're still searching, still looking for cures, still looking for miracles. Sometimes you take that right down to the end. They're not going to give up. They won't accept it. My experience is that there comes a time when you have to accept it. It's difficult. It's horrible. It's gut wrenching. It's a difficult experience to go through, but it's all part of the process of this world. You come and you go. You have to do it with as much respect and dignity and love as you can muster. Of course, every situation is different. It's reflective of the person who is ill, their personality, the way they lived their life, the way they practiced what they believed, their value system. You have to come to their base, their benchmark and work from there according to that individual. There's no common approach to this other than the basic extension of the love, the care, the concern, the comfort and availability.

18

RONALD, ROXANNE and HARRY

Ronald is the youngest of five children; his twin sister Leah having been born 10 minutes earlier. Their older brother Harry died in 1988 at the age of 42. Their oldest sister Roxanne died in 1990 at the age of 52. One older sister Amelia is still alive. Ronald is a pastor.

Harry was sick from birth. He had cerebral palsy. He was like a three-month old infant; never sat up by himself, never walked or talked. The most he ever weighed was 40 pounds. He was just a vegetable. You'd talk to him; he might smile or cry. Sometimes his eyes would follow you, but not all the time. That's why the doctor said he'd live to 10 at the most. Raising him as an infant was a struggle for Mom. She did that for 10 years, but when Leah and I were born, my parents placed Harry in an institution. My mother couldn't care for three infants. I'm sure it was hard on her. When Mom and Dad first took him there, they'd go every week to see him. Then as Harry got older, it affected him more. They would bathe him every day, but when somebody came to visit, it was their policy to bathe him and change him again. That would make him so miserable, he would just cry when Mom and Dad were there. So toward the end they just went once a month. I think it pacified Mom and Dad more than Harry.

Back then, Dad told me something I never believed until I had my own children. They had taken Harry all over the state to try to get him help. They tried chiropractors, drugs, whatever they thought would work, but nothing helped. Dad said, "If I could cut off my right arm to make Harry whole, I would do that." As a boy, I thought, "Yeah, right." Now that I have my own children, he's right.

I really didn't have a connection with Harry. I hate to say it, but when he died we almost thought it was a blessing. He just ran his course of life. There really was no grief for me personally. With Roxanne, it was different. Roxanne had a very pleasant personality and would do anything for anybody. She was 16 years older than me and married when I was 3 or 4. I don't remember too much of her being at home, but when she came back to visit, she'd take care of me like I was her kid instead of her brother. When Mom died, it was a shock. It was a grief, and I hurt. I wasn't expecting her to die, so it was tough. When Roxanne died, it was tougher.

Roxanne had very bad sugar diabetes. She was somewhat overweight, not obese, but somewhat overweight. She had a heart condition and some other health issues. But I wasn't expecting her to die, not yet, because 52 isn't really old. One day walking out of church, she had a massive heart attack. Just that quick. Being very Christian with strong faith, we like to say, "One minute she was praising God and the next minute she closed her eyes and was with God."

The day she died was very hot. She walked out of the church and started to faint. I thought she was just hot, so I asked, "Would you like some water?" She shook her head "yes." If I had known that she was going to die, I would at least have told her that I loved her. Other than that, I can't say that there were any regrets, because there were no bitter feelings, and she had lived a good life. With Harry there's a sense of regret about not having an older brother I could do things with.

Growing up Leah and I fought like cats and dogs. Now we're so close. I think the deaths, especially our mother's death, brought us closer together. Leah and I were there when Mom died, just the two of us. My dad had twisted his ankle so he didn't go to see her in the hospital that day. The day before, she had seemed ready to come home. When Leah and I got to the hospital, she was very sick. We called the doctors; they came in; said something's wrong; had us step into the hall. The next thing we heard was them calling code blue. The crash carts came. I looked over at Leah and said, "I think this is it." Sure enough it was; just that quick. A blood clot had shut everything down. The only thing she had complained of was back pain which was from the blood clot. Everything happened so quick; it was devastating. I think that bond with Leah is tighter than it ever was, because we went through that together. It's a weird thing. She lives pretty far away. Every now and then I'll call and say, "I've been thinking about this." She'll say, "So was I." It's so cool. You hear people say that, but it does really happen. Nothing major, but she'll be thinking of something and so will I. Or I'll pick up the phone to call, and she'll say, "I was getting ready to call you." I don't know if that's coincidence or not, but she's thinking to call me and I'm thinking to call her. If I lost her, I wouldn't want to say I'd be devastated, but probably I would be, at least for a while.

Losing my sister and brother has brought me closer to my other sister, too. About 2 or 3 years after Roxanne died, Amelia had a heart attack. She was in the hospital, and I was a basket case. I went in and she started crying because she saw me crying. I said, "I thought I lost you, too."

My brother's situation and then my sister's death did cause me to question my faith. But my faith was strong enough to take me past those questions. I believe that some day I will be reunited with them, one way or another. I may not know them as my brother and sister, but I will be reunited with them. I believe that when we die, that our spirit and body are reunited, that we have a glorified body. Now what that glorified body looks like, I don't know. I'm going by what I hear and read in the *Bible*, the transfiguration of Jesus. I think our bodies are going to be somewhat like that. What that was, I don't know for sure. I do believe that my brother will be whole for the very first time. Harry never had the opportunity to make a decision about religion, but I'm sure that the Good Lord will take care of him in his grace. I know where both my mother's and sister's hearts were. They believed very strongly in the Lord. So I know I will be reunited with them some day.

These experiences have helped me with my work as a minister. They've prepared me for what others are going through. When something happens to somebody, you say you feel sorry for them or you identify with it. But you can't unless you've gone through it first. I went through it with my mother and my mother-in-law. We lost a baby at 3 months along, still it's a loss. I felt the pain. I felt my wife's pain. I felt my brother and sister's pain. So I know what others are going through.

In fact, we're just starting a program at the church called HUG— Helping Understand Grief. It's still in its infancy. We want to be able to visit people in times of loss, to be there and help them. Then we want to talk to them afterwards. We're going to have monthly meetings so people can come back, and we can see how they're feeling, how they're coping, and if there is anything that we can do. One person may take a year to grieve; another person might take eight years. We want to be there for them. In this group we want to talk about living wills and maybe not being able to have children, which is also a type of grief.

One lady of the congregation was involved with a group like this years ago as part of her job. I'm not exactly sure how we started talking, but for a long time she wanted to start a group. Then last summer her husband died unexpectedly. Now she and I really want to do it. I've been through it. She was going to a support group elsewhere and said, "Let's start one within our own church." I'm really excited about it. I hope it will help people know what to say. I can say one thing to one person and it's the right thing. I can say it to the next person and it's totally wrong. You just have to be willing to deal with that. What can you really say when somebody dies. Sure there is the loss and you feel sorry for them. But they have to get over it themselves sooner or later. Or maybe they won't. Some people don't.

For people who are really strong in their faith, they are grieving because they lost someone, but there is also joy, because they know that the person went on to heaven. When people don't know the Lord, I see more sadness and grief. They're the ones that have the rougher times during funerals. When I preach a sermon at a funeral for somebody where I'm not sure where their heart lay, I sort of preach to the living, rather than too much about the deceased. I really can't help that person, but maybe I can save somebody else's soul. One of my goals in life is to get people to smile, even in the tough times, even when they are grieving. I'll say, "Well, the deceased would like what you're doing right now." Or "You could be proud of what you're doing right now." I always try to give them something to smile about; give them positive aspects.

In my own situation, we've had different experiences planning the funeral. My sisters, my father, and I planned my mother's funeral. It was a Christian service. For my sister, it was her husband and their family who planned her service. Again, it was a Christian service. For my brother, we just had a graveside service, because he was so crippled; people hadn't seen him for 30 years. Dad thought if we were at the funeral home, we'd play 30 questions all day long. So Dad felt better if we just had a graveside service.

They are all buried in Somerset. I went to the cemetery maybe 3 or 4 times a year. I had no need to go back to pacify myself, because I knew where they were. That's just a body in a grave, but it made me feel good when I put flowers on the grave. I was showing respect for them.

Our whole family is close and that's a blessing. We have family reunions on both my mom's and dad's side. They're big—100 people or more. Roxanne's husband, children and grandchildren will come. We'll get together for Christmas and Thanksgiving. We'll go to their house and visit; they'll come to our house. We call each other all the time, email. So we stay connected.

I accepted the Lord when I was in 10th grade. I was pretty passionate then. As I grew older, I kind of faded away, sowed my wild oats as they say. When I got married and started having children, I got back into the church, my faith got stronger and stronger. I was teaching youth Sunday school and held almost every office in the church. Every time I'd prepare a lesson or do a devotion, I'd feel like I was supposed to be doing something else. Something kept pulling me and telling me that I was supposed to be doing things differently. I lived that way for a year, maybe 2. I finally took the kids on a mission trip to West Virginia. We were doing some work on a house, and I was in the van going to pick up a door. The mission coordinator came up to me and said, "Why are you running away from God?" I said, "What?" He said, "Why are you running away from God? You know you're supposed to go into the ministry." I said, "Now wait a minute." I pulled the van over and we talked—after I picked my jaw off the floor. He said, "I need to tell you this. Sometimes God gives me directives. Sometimes in a dream; sometimes just feelings. If I don't answer, I can't eat. I can't sleep. I can't drink. I feel sick all over. God's been talking to me all week that I need to tell you this."

Then he goes on to tell me some stories about when this had happened to him before. "One time," he said, "a couple was trying to have children. They tried for 17 years, but nothing happened. God told me to tell them that they were going to have a baby. I fought it, but couldn't sleep or anything. So I did it. A month later they came back and they were pregnant. Another time a fellow who had been injured in the coal mines was having trouble with his disability check. It was so bad he couldn't feed his family. He was a big, burly guy, so he was going to enter a tough man competition to get money for his family. God told me to warn him not to do it; that'd he'd be injured so severely that he'd never be able to help his family. God also said the check would be in the mail on Thursday." Thursday it was in his mailbox."

Those were pretty powerful stories. Then he said, "God says you need to get into the ministry." I'd been kicking things around, because I knew something wasn't right in my life. So I talked it over with my wife and a few people and prayed. I just kept going forward and getting into the ministry.

I grew up in a religious family. I knew through studies and what I'd been told, that sooner or later, you have a decision to make;

whether you're going to give your life to the Lord or not; which ultimately determines where you spend eternity. In 10th grade we had a lay witness mission in our church where people came from all over the state, even out of state. They talked about how their lives changed through the Lord. That's when I made my commitment to accept Jesus as my personal savior. I said, "I'm a sinner. I accept your forgiveness through grace."

I was 22 when I got married; we had our first kid when we were 27 or 28. I already knew where my faith was, but I got to thinking. My mom and dad had us in church every week. It was a good thing for me; I turned out semi-decent. I thought it was a good example for my kids. So that's when I really started getting committed. As I got in there, people could see where my faith was and that I knew a little bit about the scriptures. They started getting me to teach and deal with the youth, which I really enjoyed. In fact, I was youth director for 15 years. Every time I prepared a lesson geared to those kids, I thought, "I need to be doing something different than this." I didn't know what, but I had this feeling. Even when I'd do my own personal daily devotions, I'd get these vibes. Something was calling me to do something different. I guess God used that fellow to tell me what it was.

I never thought five years ago I'd be a pastor. I was a manager of a hardware store; before that I was the manager of a super market. But the church was still moving in my work, because people knew that I was a Christian and would talk differently around me than they would around other people. Every chance I had, I would tell people about my faith. I've been a pastor for a year and a half. I'm going to seminary right now. There are different types of pastorals you can get into. You can be a full ordained elder; you can be a deacon in the church; you can be a local pastor. Because of my age, I'm going the local pastor route for now. Maybe I'll become a fully ordained elder later, but right now I've got to get my kids through college. So I'm just taking the local pastor route, which doesn't make much difference, other than the title. I'm not in it for the title. I'm in it to serve God.

It was a hard adjustment for me when I got to be a pastor. One day I was the manager of a hardware store and the next day I was the pastor of four churches. This is a big church. The other three are very small. But one day I'm Ronald; the next day I'm Pastor Ronald to everybody. They see me as their representative of God. That was difficult for me to learn. The strangest part is with my dad and sisters. They see me as Ronald who likes to have a good time; Ronald who plays practical jokes. They don't see me as a pastor. It's nice to be with them, because I can let my hair down.

I have been enjoying this, tremendously. Even with all the extra school work on top of my regular duties, everything has been going well. I think that is confirmation that God has me doing what I'm supposed to be doing. Whenever I was going through this, I would ask my wife, "What do you think I should do?" She wouldn't tell me; she wanted me to make up my own mind. Once I was moving forward, she said, "I think that's what you need to be doing. I'm behind you 110%." It meant a lot that she wouldn't try to sway me one way or the other.

We need to share experiences of loss like this. How we grieve, losing a sibling is clearly different than losing a mother or a father. I think we need to know how to grieve; what to tell people; how to react. How I feel. How you feel. We need to do that.

If Leah would die that might change my identity a little bit, because I talk to her a lot. In fact I talk to her about stuff that I wouldn't talk to my wife about. Like about this ministry thing. After I talked to my wife and she wouldn't give me a decision one way or the other, I went to my sister. She said she could see it, too. That's just one thing; many things; more things within the family about Dad and Mom that I wouldn't talk about with my wife. It's odd, but my twin's name is the same as my wife's name. I've lived in a house with someone named Leah since the day I was born.

19

KENDRA, BRENT and TRISH

Kendra is the oldest of four siblings. Her brother Brent died in 1988 at the age of 38. Kendra was 44 at the time. Kendra's sister, Trish was diagnosed with a very virulent form of cancer in the summer of 2001. She died in December of that year at the age of 50. The forth sibling, Drew, is six and a half years younger than Kendra.

Brent and I were Irish twins, meaning that we were only 11 months apart. We were very close. Alita, his wife, was diagnosed with stage-4 brain cancer shortly after their daughter, Lee, was born. Alita went through chemotherapy, but died about two years later at the age of 28. Brent really adored his daughter and spent as much time as he possibly could with her.

Brent was a very dashing guy. He had a motorcycle and a dirt bike. When Lee was 9, Brent was riding his motorcycle about 12:30 at night. There had been a light rain and the roads were slick. Apparently he skidded off the road, hit a guardrail, and was killed instantly. His neck snapped. My husband and I got a call about 3:00 in the morning. My husband went right away to get Lee. Brent had taken the babysitter for a ride on the bike, so Lee was alone. The babysitter had a hurt hand.

We had been designated as Lee's guardians so we raised her as our daughter. I have three sons. All are two years apart. Lee was the fourth, and again, 2 years younger than my youngest son. That's been a very joyous, very wonderful thing for us. Life went on. Not a day goes by that I don't think of Brent. But after the initial shock and hurt, I was fortunate enough to focus on Lee. My children were really terrific. They were encouraged to be inclusive, and they were. So she really had, I think, a very good childhood and upbringing. She's 23 now and seems to be a very well adjusted, lovely woman.

My sister Trish lived in Virginia. She was a sailor and raced small boats. In June of 2001, she had a twinge in her abdomen, but thought it was just an ache or a pain. She thought she might have just nudged a rib or something while she was on the boat. On July 4th, she really didn't feel well. Trish was divorced and had one son. She'd been dating one guy for about three years, and he said, "I'd better take you to the hospital." At the hospital they started this x-ray process. Initially, they thought it was cancer of the liver; then they thought maybe it was the kidney. On September 10, oddly enough just prior to 9/11, Trish went through a long surgery. They took out her right kidney, gall bladder, appendix, part of her pancreas. At that point we knew that the cancer was virulent.

I went to stay with her for several weeks. She was not comfortable. We got her into Johns Hopkins and they started chemotherapy even though this type of cancer does not respond to chemo or radiation. We had been warned that in order to have a shot at saving her, she'd need chemo. Plus, the chemo could also help to manage the pain. She was on a morphine pump and a feeding tube. In the end, she actually had only two doses of chemo, but it was so strong her heart just gave out. She actually died of a heart attack, which was a blessing since she wasn't going to make it.

Trish's death was so much harder for me than Brent's. Brent's death was a shock, but I don't have any mental images of what happened. It was mitigated somewhat by the fact that I had his lovely little girl that I could put my attention to. With Trish, I watched her die. That's much harder. I can't help but review her courage. I remember the poignant moments about her losing her hair. She was just a skeleton. Trish's son is 20. I'm in constant touch with him. The whole family is; we care very much for him. He's in school in Virginia. It's not like you can just put him under your wing. So for sure, Trish's death was worse.

The human mind is such a protective thing. Even though we all knew in our gut she was dying, we were shocked when she died so suddenly from the heart attack. We had expected that she would continue to live here. I slept in the same room with her so I could monitor what was happening. Frankly it's grueling, but I wouldn't have had it any other way. When she died, I just thought to myself, somebody has spared her the rest of this. As much as it was so painful to know that she was no longer here, in my heart I really knew that that was better for her.

She was so fabulous. I don't think I ever saw her cry. She remained very much herself. She was a comptroller for Stuckey's Corp for 24 years; had a very mathematical, business type mind. A no nonsense type, although a great deal of fun. She had a great sense of humor. Just all around a wonderful sister. She always seemed to have her wits about her, even when she was on morphine. I saw only a few, very minimal effects from the morphine; just small lapses of judgment that one could understand in her circumstances. She very often didn't feel well. I mean when you're sick to your stomach, you don't really feel up to yourself.

The night before she died had not been good; she had nausea. But the next morning, she woke up and was more bright-eyed and said, "I think this is going to be a good day." I went to get myself a cup of coffee. I got her a tiny glass of ginger ale. We were sitting and just chatting about the day. She seemed good. Her TPN wasn't finished yet—that's a bag of nutrients that's specially formulated and it goes in through ports in the vein. It takes over 12 hours for it to go through. She was always antsy in the morning, wanting to get that off. That morning I said, "You've got to finish this. You've got 110 units left out of 900." So it was enough that she needed to finish, which would take about an hour.

At the time, most of my kids were home for Christmas break. My oldest son needed a ride to a nearby town to pick up a car. I said,

"I'm going to run out for ½ hour." She asked, "Can I take this out?" I said, "No, you've never done it. I'll be back in half an hour. I'll split it with you. If you agree to stay on this for another half hour, I'll give you leeway on the other half hour. You won't have to finish it." On the way back from dropping my son off, my youngest son called. "Mom, I think Trish is having a heart attack. I've called 911." Three EMTs were there when I got home, but she was dead before she left the house. They couldn't get a pulse. They couldn't do anything.

She had tried to disconnect the feeding tube. She had never done it before; I always did it. To disconnect the TPN, you had to clamp the valve on the vena cava for the shunt. Trish had forgotten to do that. This is one of the areas where the morphine clouded her judgment. It was a momentary mistake and then it frightened her. There was blood on the bed. I think it scared her, and her heart was so weak that it gave out. She should have waited for me to come home, because then that wouldn't have happened. On the other hand you think, "Maybe it was just God's way of saying, you don't have to do this anymore." Maybe Trish didn't believe that she was as sick as she was. Not that she would recover, but that she had more time.

Trish had the most incredible amount of family support. She was never left alone. Even at Johns Hopkins where they see this all the time, they were astounded. If there was a doctor's meeting, everybody was there. I would drive back and forth to Baltimore in one day. Her boyfriend Kurt was also there. Her son Ashton was unbelievable. He moved up here for a couple of weeks, then commuted back home. She really had the most incredible environment around her in terms of us.

Her quality of life was as good as it could be. It wasn't so bad that even two weeks before she died, we got her a wheel chair and went to Staples to buy my mother a fax machine. A guy was there who didn't know what to buy. Trish, having been a businesswoman, had such a good time helping him figure out which fax machine he needed. She was smart, intellectual. I think there was quality to her life.

I also think everything is relative. If you are as sick as she was, perhaps you don't realize that you aren't sailing or racing your sailboat. She slowly but surely had begun to adjust to her illness. If it was a good day, it was a good day just because she felt good; didn't have nausea or something else. If she didn't feel well, she just slept. I can't say that her quality of life was really awful. There was always something to look forward to.

Drew and I have been a wonderful support system for each other. These losses have been devastating. We were a very, very close, wonderful family. Sometimes I wonder, "How did this ever happen? How can we go from four to two?" I think I'm more attentive to him, more thoughtful. He's the same with me. We get along very well. We always have. So it's not like our relationship has changed, but it's just that we're down to two, and it's a shock.

I do ask why this happened to them. It just seems so remarkable to me. We have never had health problems. We lived in the country. We've been active. It just doesn't seem possible that they would be gone. I still have a real trouble with Trish. She wanted to be cremated and wanted her ashes spread either in the Gulf Stream or the Chesapeake Bay." That hasn't been done yet, because she died in December and it hasn't been possible. I wake up in the middle of the night, thinking where's Trish? I need some anchor spot for her. Some people are looser about it; they can deal with no place to go. My husband's father was cremated. He was a golfer so some of his ashes are sprinkled in Pine Valley and some here. That would never do for me. I want a mental image, if nothing else an old oak tree; it just needs to be there for me.

With Brent, we planted his favorite tree, a white oak, in the churchyard. We had a plaque made. His grave is next to his wife's and my father's. The American Arborist Association established a memorial fund for Brent, which supports training programs for young arborists. It was the great love of his life and he was very good at it. For Trish, there's a memorial fund at Johns Hopkins set up particularly for sarcoma cancers, because they're the hardest; they're the worst. She had many friends in Morton, VA, and I think they're going to plant a tree for her. But see that's what has been bothering me. Right now, she's in an urn at the funeral home. I don't want to sound like I can't be imaginative enough to know that Trish is with us in spirit. I understand that part. But there's something about me that needs an anchor. My husband and I bought the family farm where I grew up. I have a little garden that I'm redoing. When I learned about Trish, I'd been thinking about this garden all along. It's going to be Trish's garden. I'll ask her son Ashton if I can have a handful of her ashes, so I can bury them in this little garden.

We grew up and were confirmed in the Presbyterian Church. Religion has never been overdone in our family. It is just one of the things that we do. We went to Sunday school. We go to church, but that's the extent of it. We certainly believe in God and in good things for people who died. We don't think of someone as being tormented. We think of it as a place of being at peace. We realize that our feelings are connected to our missing someone rather than it being a terrible thing for them. We understand what we've been taught about religion. I'm very grateful for it; it's a very great anchor.

I think about the Trade Center bombings and people who, just out of the blue, lost someone. I think about the horrendous things that have happened to people in Afghanistan. We're all part of a bigger picture of humanity. So many people suffer such incredible, horrible things. At least those in my family, who have died, have died surrounded by family. There's a great deal of peace in that for me.

I've gotten a little apprehensive. My children are very adventurous and have been encouraged to be. I've got one who is a tall-ship sailor who has been around the world for two years. I've got one who just got back from a seminar in Cuba. They rock climb, mountain climb, and mountain bike. Every now and then I have to take a deep breath and think, "It's better to have really lived, than to be so meek." I keep telling myself that, because that's the way I've always felt. I'm a foxhunter; I've done ocean racing and things like that myself. But I've gotten a little more fearful. I think that will go away. It hasn't been that long.

I recognize where the anxiety comes from; I understand it; I'm not denying it. Giving myself permission to have it is a normal thing. We're not foolish people, but there is a lot of life to be lived. I'd rather live as I need to live than to be worried about whether I'm going to break my toe or have a car accident. There is a little bit of the fatalist in me. There is a bigger design, and I don't get to be in charge. I do have to go from the intellectual to the emotional. That is a balance. I know that this will dissipate. My oldest son bought himself a big fancy motorcycle, but didn't want to tell me. He knew that I'd lost my brother. When he brought it home, I knew it was the most exciting moment in the whole world for him. So one night I came down—it took me a little time—and I said "Jeff, good for you. I'm proud for you. You've worked hard. You could afford this nice bike. You know my anxieties about this. I just trust you to be careful; just be prudent." He said, "Mom, I know so well, and I'm glad you came to me. I wanted it in the worst way, but..." It just opened up the dialog. He's 29. He's not disobeying me. What control do I have over that? But he didn't want to hurt me. So it meant a lot for me to say, "It's fine. It's fine."

Our family doctor, whom we've known for 40 some years, is wonderful. I called him after I knew Trish's diagnosis. He said, "Kendra, this is not good." I asked him, "Ed, I need to talk to mother about this whole thing. She's fragile right now. My instinct is to shoot straight with her." He said, "Go with your instincts." So I did. I sat down with her. I spent a lot of time with her. I had done the same thing when my father was ill. Dr. Ed would come to me and say, "Kendra, this is really, really not good." I was the one who would have to say, "Mother, we're at a bad place." I was able to trust that I could tell my mother the truth, which is to her credit.

I said, "Mother, you know our family has always had courage. We're going to go on. We're going to do everything we can do, but here are the circumstances. We're just going to go forward. We're going to find the best advice we can; put Trish in the best place we can; do everything that we can do. And that's the best we can do." My mother latched on to that and said, "You're right. We will just go ahead and carry on." I think that held her together. You know, with the old *esprit de corps*. That worked.

We had a moment of hope after Trish's first chemo treatment. We had been told it would do no good, but it managed not just to diminish the cancer, but also to contain it. So we thought that the 2nd chemo might diminish it further. That was a small ray of hope. I think the medical community gets together and says, "Look, we've got to offer hope. The human mind is such a powerful thing that we can't tell the patients, they're done for." They tell the truth as you would to a young child. Give the basics, because you've got to be truthful, but say, "We have these possibilities." One time when a team of doctors came around, I did say to them, "I think it's important for you to let me know for sure that there is no hope." They did, but we discussed it. When you lose hope, you've lost a very positive thing. Hope needs to surround everybody, even though the truth was lurking in the back of my mind, in everybody's mind, in my sister's mind. Trish was no fool. It wasn't a charade, but there was her getting up and saying, "This is going to be a good day." Those kinds of things are very positive, and I do believe in the human mind. I do think that there are times when people prevail. If this had happened to me, I don't know that I could have been as unbelievably great as Trish. Maybe that's a natural thing to think. I guess we deal when we have to. We do whatever we have to. You do keep your sanity. You do even keep your sense of humor. I don't think you can predict how you'll react.

Trish's death has been the hardest one for me, because I watched her and tried so hard to help her. I didn't have a chance to try with Brent. I tried hard with my father, but he was an older man. In a sense his life had been blessed; he had done everything; it was time. We could put some peace to that. It didn't mean that it was any better, but it was not as horrendous as watching and being helpless. You never know. It may or may not be easier. There are a lot of tools that people can use and perspective is one of them. It's better to have been with someone. You can't control their disease, but at least you can help. Some people don't get the chance; people whose children are raped; just horrible things. When one thinks about it, they're just twisted. It happens all over the world; in the Middle East; it's happening as we speak. There's wisdom in looking at a big picture, and feeling grateful for the things that didn't happen.

A lot can be uplifting during this time. Find a funny card. Do things that you wouldn't normally do. Just seize the moment, because it will be gone. You do not want to have any regrets. I'm grateful that I could sleep night after night with Trish and get up in the middle of the night with her and have some laughs. I mean like, "Where are you going with that IV pole. You're banging into everything." We would laugh. Trish lost her hair, and one day we couldn't quite shave the whole head. So we went for a haircut, and it was hysterical. We both got to laughing. I mean what are you going to do? You're either going to laugh or you're going to cry. Little things. Little vanity things—special creams, a pretty little blouse. Her eyesight got bad so I'd read to her; not necessarily anything profound; not necessarily funny. Just fun stuff; just trying to be as normal as possible. I'd call her and say, "Now, Trish, here's a situation. What would you do?" She loved that; loved being important. There are funny things and proud things. Trish was so proud of her son Ashton. We would talk about that. We could reminiscence. When Ashton was a little boy, he would spend time with me; get on a pony; it was like Camp Kendra. We would reminisce about that. Talk about what a great kid he turned out to be. That kind of warmth. It didn't always have to be about the fear of death. Those are things I gave her, that were really worthwhile to her. She was happy to be able to respond.

We would talk about the necessity of getting things in order, like a will and taking her ex-husband off a life insurance policy. Fortunately, my brother Andrew took over those types of things, because I wouldn't have been much help.

Trish never expressed a fear of dying. After she died, I thought, "Is this going to happen to me? Am I going to get this cancer? Am I going to die the same way?" That goes back to my anxiety. Maybe it's irrational, but that's the truth. Trish never expressed fear. She would be extremely attentive when the home-care nurses would show us how to do something like the feeding tube. It was no problem for me, because I had done that with my father. Trish would be sure she understood something, but the morphine would cloud her judgment. I'm good at understanding directions. I'd have to say, "No, Trish, this is the way we do it." Finally to assuage her, I put something on my computer. Step one. Step two. Step three. Her anxiety was focused on a port that she had in the top of her chest, going into her superior vena cava. She worried about little details, but never said anything about her mortality. I just knew it was not right to ask, "Are you afraid of dying?" The reason, I think, was that the whole *modus operandi* of the doctors was "let's keep trying." Because she knew of the family devotion, Trish said "I'm going to fight this as best as I can." She was worried about us.

One day I was on my way to Virginia, when I got a call that they were taking Trish to Alexandria for some type of infusion. When I took her home later that night, I said, "Trish, listen. This is not right. We're going to Hopkins." I had tried before to get her to go, but Trish had her own mind. I said, "Trish, forgive me, but I'm going to take the bull by the horns, because you're not well." She said, "It sounds good to me."

When I got back home, her significant other accused me of trying to kidnap Trish. That was fairly traumatic to me. I was just trying to help her. I had arranged an ambulance, because she was in pain. I went up to her bedroom and said, "Trish, I want to be sure this is what you want me to do. I'm not trying to run your life, but you need to be somewhere that people can help you. Enough of this Maalox over the counter stuff. This is trouble. We need to get you somewhere." She agreed. She did look to me for help. That's a hard part. To take the bull by the horns and say, "You're out of here. We're going to do this." In those times she knew that she wasn't well. I hope that if I were in Trish's shoes a member of my family would say, "Kendra, we're going to get you where you need to be." I spent practically every day with her. When you do that, you really get to see what's going on.

I don't dream much about Brent anymore. Frankly, I think the experience of his death was different for me, partly because I put my heart and soul into Lee. It was such a job to ensure that she was cared for; working with my own children to make her world what it should be. Also, maybe it was partly that time in my life. Brent was 38; I was 39. I was still in the throes of raising our kids; I had a barn full of horses; lots of activities. It was different with Trish; maybe because I spent so many nights with her; listening for a warning buzzer to go off; getting up to fix it a twisted tube or cord. Maybe it is also the struggle of her death and the fact that we don't have a place for her yet. For some reason it is important to me that Trish has a little spot of her own on this earth.

20

KATE, BILL and DON

Kate is the second of four children. She had an older brother Don and two younger brothers—twins Henry and Bill. Growing up, Kate and Don seemed like one sibling group and the twins like another. Kate's father died very young and her mother raised the four children on her own.

Bill, the younger twin (the "baby" of the family) died at the age of 43 in the September 8, 1994 crash of US Airways flight 427. Don died in November 2000 at the age of 55 from complications following a colonoscopy. Kate's mother died three weeks after Don. When I spoke with Kate in 2001, she said in some ways the crash seemed like a lifetime ago and in other ways it seemed like now, because the details of that evening are crystal clear.

It was a Thursday evening and I heard something on the news about a plane crash. At first they said it was a plane leaving Pittsburgh for Chicago. I didn't give it more thought than thinking how terrible that was. The announcement was flashing on the TV, but they didn't have any details like whether there were any survivors. I went to bed about 9:00. I wasn't asleep, but just resting in bed when the phone rang; it was Don. He said, "Have you been watching the news?" I said, "No. I saw something earlier about a plane crash." He was real quiet and then said, "We think Bill was on the plane." I said, "No. The plane was going <u>to</u> Chicago." Don said, "No. It was coming <u>from</u> Chicago." Bill traveled there frequently on business, but I didn't know exactly when he was coming or going. If I had known he was coming home, I would have paid more attention.

I had a picture of him by the bed, and I was hugging it; just holding on to something. I called down to Faith [her partner] that Bill was on the plane. I started crying and Faith was horrified. I was in my pajamas and just threw something on because we had to go over to my mother's in Mt. Washington and tell her what happened. My nephew who was in medical school in Philadelphia happened to be in town, and his girlfriend had just started school at the University of Pittsburgh. So we picked her up in Oakland and met him at my mother's. We pushed the buzzer and the first person my mother saw when she opened the door was my nephew. Her face lit up and she said, "Oh, hello! Wow!" Then she saw the rest of us and it was like, "What's going on? Why are you here?" You could see the look come over her face even though she didn't know what it was. I don't know if she had seen anything about the crash on TV, but even if she had, it wasn't connected to anything. We told her and she just started wailing.

Bill and Henry were very close and talked pretty much every day on the phone. Henry knew that Bill had been in Chicago and was coming home. He called Bill's wife Tammy. I guess a neighbor happened to be at her house and answered the phone. He must have sounded like Bill, because at first Henry had this flood of relief and was saying, "Thank God; thank God. You're okay." When he realized it wasn't Bill, he knew that Bill had probably been on the plane. Even still, your mind keeps having all these contradictory thoughts like maybe he had to stay another day or maybe he decided to drive home. Even as we're having those thoughts, we knew Bill would have called to say he was alright. The plane crashed about 7:00 pm. Bill would have called immediately to let us know he was okay. You have these contradictory thoughts to keep some hope.

Henry went over to be with Tammy. We stayed at my mother's. Then began the nightmare of trying to get confirmation. We were calling the airline continuously, but we couldn't get through. When we finally did get through, they wouldn't tell us anything until they checked the passenger list. They have a list of people who made reservations, but they don't know right away who was actually on the plane. We didn't get confirmation until 3:00 in the morning. They called Tammy and then she or Henry called us. My mother was wailing and wailing and wailing.

I think a self-protective thing happens that helps you get over not having the opportunity to say goodbye. It doesn't cover up the terrible, unbelievable pain. It was hardest on Tammy; not being able to say goodbye. She'd cry and say, "I just want to hold him one more time and tell him I love him."

Bill had two children. His daughter was 14 and had just started high school. His son was just 11. I don't remember the details about all of the phone calls back and forth. Someone had call their house and she was like," Is that Dad on the phone?" She went to her room and started shaking. At one point I went up to her room and she said, "He'll never see me graduate. He'll never see me get married. He'll never hear about my first day at high school." She was crystal clear about the impact of what was lost. She wasn't just suffering now; she was suffering for all that was lost in the future. They were very close. He was very involved with so many of her activities.

My brothers and I always thought we would grow old together. We knew my mother would go one day. My father was already gone. The twins had each other. I did more with my older brother Don; had the closest emotional connection with him. But we had this sense that we would always be there with each other. We had always been there. This was the first time, I thought, "Oh my God, what am I supposed to do now? You were supposed to be with me." I don't have a husband or children so I counted on my brothers to be there as I got older. There's also something about how brothers and sisters carry the history of your family, your life.

You don't really want to know about airplane safety. It's so corrupt, so obscene, so criminal; you just want to take the whole system down. The 737 is the most frequently used aircraft in the industry. There have been at least five incidents with the rudder. They know what to do with it, but they haven't fixed it. I think now there is an agreement to do something over the next four or five years, but they're in no rush. They've done a cost-benefit analysis and figure it costs less to pay the families of victims than it would be to fix the planes.

I can't think about it a lot because I get too angry. I wasn't a Pollyanna about these things. I know there are all sorts of products with defects that don't get fixed. It doesn't come as a total surprise. But so much of my energy goes into my personal grief, I can't take that on as a cause. Some do. One of the things that was unusual about this crash is the number of people from the same community. Usually when there is a crash the passengers are from all over. This was a commuter flight so there were a lot of people from Pittsburgh: businessmen, executives, etc. Some of their families have formed a group and are crusading for changes. They have been instrumental in getting legislation passed so that now the airlines have to appoint a family advocate at the time of a crash who is separate from the airline. This is someone who works on behalf of the families, who can serve as a liaison, and get them information. Early on, the airlines are thinking, "We don't want people suing." So they assign someone to interact with families. They pull someone like a ticket agent and tell them, "You are assigned to this family and this family and this family." They are not trained. Even if they're a good person, they're overwhelmed and horrified, too. Thank God the first person we had turned out to be a wonderful human being. Lots of families had horror stories. Our next person was okay. She knew the business end of it, but was pretty much of a cold fish.

Right after the crash, the airlines will fly in family members if they are out of town; put them up in a hotel. They'll pay for the funeral. They do that right away, but it isn't too long afterward that they start sending out surveys, trying to get the lay of the land. It's just seedy after a while. And then of course attorneys come out of the woodwork, from across the country, who start calling. An attorney from Louisiana kept calling; I told him to stop. I filed a complaint.

Tammy and Henry became part of a smaller support group and went to meetings for a couple of years. A lot of people in that group are still really close and will do family things together. That helped them. We went to a national disaster meeting where we met people from all these different crashes. You think your story is the worst but then you can't imagine what you hear. One woman lost her husband in a plane crash, remarried and lost her second husband in a plane crash. Just when you think the absolute worst thing in the world happened to you, it's topped constantly by these worse horrors. It helps put things in perspective, meeting people, talking with them.

Tammy did eventually enter a lawsuit. As a sibling I had no standing. You have to be a parent, a child, or a spouse. Probably something might have been worked out, but it isn't automatic. It's like the sibling relationship isn't as important. I was angry about that. Not that I wanted to get money. It's the sense of "What am I? Chopped liver?"

Tammy wanted me to go with her to the attorney. We had to find an attorney; figure out how to get started in the process; had to talk with several. It was hard because every time we had to tell the story, it brought up the feelings and we'd cried. We did eventually find someone who had a lot of experience with wrongful death lawsuits. He teared up when we told him the story. It was Tammy's decision, but we both felt we wanted someone we could talk to and he wouldn't be like a disgusting shark. Yet you want someone who will really fight for you. The airlines have the advantage over you; millions of dollars; lawyers coming out the wazoo. They dig into your victim's life; not to completely eliminate a payment, but to cut off another million or a half dollars. If one person didn't work as hard as other people, they can devalue the person's productivity to the jury. The whole thing was geared toward scaring you into settling. Tammy didn't have any heart for going to court. She did have in mind a certain figure. Of course, there is no way of knowing what to ask. You keep that to yourself. You don't sit around with the other families asking, "What are you willing to settle for?" The settlement is based in part on future earnings and that's very different for everyone. Talking about it in these terms is very strange.

There really is a contrast between Bill's and Don's death. With Bill there was a tremendous outpouring of sympathy from the entire region. Everyone knew about it; it seemed almost like they took it on as their own grief and suffered with you. That's one of the things that helped us get through it. I had cards and flowers, and people from everywhere identified with the loss. I drew comfort and strength from every card, every flower, every expression of sympathy. People whose loved ones died in crashes outside of Pittsburgh talked about this. They had to deal with the grief all by themselves. I think it made a difference for us to get through it with all the support, knowing thousands and thousands of people were sad for us. I've told people since then, "If you ever wonder what difference a card can make, don't minimize it. Because every little expression told me people cared and that would take away a few more ounces of the pain." I appreciated people who would talk about it and let me shed some tears and then go on. I understood that some people can't do that, because they don't know what to say or do; they're scared. They think that if you cry, they made it worse. They haven't; it's just part of the process.

I have to say it was different when Don died. Of the four of us, Don was the one who was medically vulnerable. He had had a kidney transplant and was on disability. But he was medically stable and there was no sense of imminent death. He went for a routine colonoscopy. A day or so later he began to feel ill. His intestine had been punctured during the procedure; he was developing a major infection in his abdomen. An operation was done on Wednesday to eradicate the infection. After this operation, he did not seem right to the family, but the physicians kept saying that he was okay. Over the course of three or four days his condition continued to worsen to the point that the physicians became concerned. By the weekend, there was major concern that he might not recover, but they could not locate any infection. He was on antibiotics, but was not responding. By Monday, the family was told that he would probably not make it through the day. He held on for two more days but was unconscious. The family approved taking him off life support on Wednesday and he died that day or the next. We had all been there with him. He wasn't really able to respond, but there was this sense of being able to say goodbye. It's not like people didn't care, but it was much more private. People around me, even people who knew me pretty well, didn't necessarily know how close I was to Don. My relationship with him was such an integral part of my life; I'd talk to him almost every day. He'd pop over to visit. He wasn't physically strong, but he'd come over and help me in whatever way he could.

So people expressed sympathy but it was different than knowing a whole region was mourning with us. The pain of the losses is easing over time. Not that it's less intense. I still feel the grief intensely, but it's not all the time, not every day.

Visiting the crash site was painful, but did bring some comfort about Bill's death. The need to visit was partly because we didn't have a chance to say good-bye. There's a sense that part of him is there or that's the last place that he was. The first time we went was about a week or so after the crash, I didn't know what to expect. You get to the crash site on a little dirt road that goes through a ravine. The walls are maybe 15 feet high and then the road opens into a relatively small area. A 737 is very large; it would have filled the entire space if it had just landed. The plane came in at an angle and hit the very top of this ravine. The nose hit into that small space and the plane exploded on impact. Airplane parts were in the trees, all over the ground, over a wide area. I picked up a couple of pieces of the plane. I wasn't expecting that. I thought the whole area would have been cleaned up. Clearly they had done everything they could to get body parts out of there, but there was debris everywhere.

It was very painful to see the crash site. We cried again. We just cried endlessly for a few months; just endlessly. But there was something else; the site took on a sort of spiritual quality. We went on a Sunday and there was a young man wandering around. Tammy struck up a conversation with him. His wife had been on the plane. He lived in Chicago and had driven in to spend about 15 minutes at the site before driving back home. It was so weird that we would be there in that same short time and that Tammy talked to him. I mean we usually didn't talk to other people. It turns out his wife had been sitting next to my brother. This was extremely comforting for all of us. As he talked about his wife, she sounded like a young, energetic, pretty (he had pictures of her), friendly, outgoing, all around wonderful human being. Bill was also extremely outgoing and friendly. We knew that they would have talked. One of the worst things was thinking about the last 43 seconds as the plane was descending. You can just picture this horror. It was comforting to know that he had somebody. They would have grabbed each other's hands or held each other and would have comforted each other somehow. It meant something that he was next to her. There was really this feeling that he found somebody and she had somebody and it was comforting.

I used to be religious. I was a nun so of course religion was a big part of my life for many, many years. I lost it when I came out of the convent and never regained my faith. For many people, they draw their strength and comfort from their faith. It isn't for me. People say, "You'll see Bill again in heaven." I don't know. Maybe. It's sort of hard for me to believe. If I could believe that, it would cut my suffering in half. It wouldn't go away, but if you really think that when you die you're going to go up there and see all your family, that's not so bad. My sisters-in-law believe that and it helps them. Especially Don's wife who is much more devout. Tammy believes she's going to see Bill. She's not super religious, but she did draw comfort from that.

For some people there was the whole thing about remains. For me, I didn't care. He was gone. Body parts or body, I don't need that. In fact, I'd rather not know any more about it. Tammy had to have something back that was identified, because she had to have a burial spot. Although the crash happened on a beautiful, clear, Fall evening, it rained later that night; not hard, not long, but it did rain. That bothered me—that he was out there by himself in the rain. I thought, "Who cares? What does it matter?" For some reason, though, it just did me in.

We did get some of Bill's things back. It was bizarre. One of the things we were told was to cancel his credit cards, because there were looters out there. I was the one who cancelled the credit cards. Tammy was hoping for his high school class ring. It was important to Bill and she wanted to give it to her son, but it never came back. Then you wonder if someone stole it. What did come back was his money clip that had this plastic thing on it that Bill's son had given him a few years earlier. Bill always used it even though he could afford a more expensive one. You have to help me understand how something like that survived the impact of the crash. His wallet didn't come back, but some family pictures, including my high school graduation picture, weren't burned. How did these things come out of such a conflagration? People will tell you there is no rhyme or reason for what wasn't destroyed. I went once to the place where they had laid things out. It was very creepy. All these personal belongings were laid out; the plane parts were laid out in a huge hanger. We were taken to see that. We got to see his seat. It was like you go into an altered state. I wasn't going to go, but then everyone else was, so I went, too. It was bizarre. There were really just little shreds that they had laid out.

Two days after Bill died, I went through all my pictures from when we were kids on up. I made a little album and took it over to Tammy. I realized I didn't really have anything in writing from him. Because we both lived here, we didn't write letters. Then I remembered that when I went into the convent, which was 30 years to the day, both Bill and Don had written me notes. I frantically went through things and I did find those. They were very precious.

I wouldn't say there are specific, special memories that stand out, but there are flashes of things; his sweetness, friendliness. There were a lot of pleasant memories of Bill. Don was not sweetness and pleasantness. After you got to know him, you could see he had a very tender side to him, but he had a harder exterior; was harder to get to know. You had to work your way in and then you're in forever. I think I had a special relationship with Don because he didn't open up as easily to other people. For Don, I was a little sister at first, but then a peer as we got older. Someone he could talk with. I'm not sure he talked with a lot of other people, including his wife. Overall I think we had a very special relationship.

Henry is struggling more than any of us. I don't think he'll ever get over losing Bill. Being twins, they were so close. He talks about this giant hole that can never be filled. He was angry at God. While he was friendly, he wasn't as friendly as Bill, wasn't as comfortable with himself as Bill. Didn't have the confidence level that Bill had. Losing Bill did him in. Then losing Don. He's so angry. I don't know how to help him. I wish he would talk with someone, but he won't do it. He talks to me a little, but not easily, so I can go only so far. Maybe I should push him more or keep in touch more. It doesn't come as easily because I didn't have that kind of relationship with him.

I hope Henry and I can keep working on this together, because his wife comes from a long line of stoics and seems to feel that you grieve for a while and then get over it. I think she's had it with his involvement in the support group. I feel bad that she isn't as supportive as he might need. He insisted that he didn't want to celebrate his birthday. It was their birthday and now it's only his, and it's close to the date of the crash. The first year after the crash his wife had some friends over for dinner; we gave him a few gifts which was okay. After that he kept saying he didn't want to celebrate. The year he turned 50, he really dug his heels in and absolutely insisted that he didn't want anything. Finally, I said to him, "It's not just for you. It's for us, too. We're damn grateful you're here since a lot of people are gone." In the end, there was no party. A week or so after his birthday, I did give him a small gift. By then he was calmed down a bit, but he said, "Next year do nothing; I'm done with it."

For Bill there was an official memorial and a ceremony on the anniversary of the crash. A lot of people were around; cameramen from all the news stations. There was still a sense of being surrounded by a community that cares. With Don, it was different. I took the day off; we all went to the cemetery. That's the first time I had been back, and we sort of relived the whole thing. Then we went home, played some games, and went out to dinner; made a day of it. This was on a Thursday, the day he had died. But I actually started reliving what had happened on Sunday and each day leading up to his death.

Don and I always went out for dinner on Sunday. On Monday I took him for his tests, etc. Wednesday before he died had been my final day with him. So by Thursday when we went to the cemetery I had been crying all week; going through my own personal process. When Thursday came, it was a relief; the worst part was over for me. I don't know what we will do next year, but that helped me get through this year.

It's taken a long time, but I think I'm doing better now. I have more feelings of happiness. These deaths affected my sense of self. So much of my identity was tied up with family, especially Don. If I'm not in daily contact with him anymore and I don't have my mother anymore, what does this make me; who am I; what is my life now? You have a picture of what your life is, even if it is unconscious. Now it's not going along that way. That was a big thing for me; kind of scary. I had to re-invent myself, figure out what I am. It's not who I thought I would be. I was mad about that and scared. I still don't have a final sense of that, but you just go on. All my relationships are disrupted and that was big for me because I'm not married and don't have children. For me, those sibling relationships were the big relationships, the permanent relationships. Society looks at the marital relationship as primary, but that's not the case for me. If you have children there would be a sense of someone being there as you grow old or who you leave behind. Don's children are close to me and that is comforting.

With Don there was a complete sense of belonging. Whatever I would do; wherever I would be; there was never a question that I would absolutely have a place with him. He was the only person I felt completely safe with, which is ridiculous because physically he wasn't any stronger than I was. But I could be in his presence and completely relax. I don't feel that way with anyone else in the world. I can ask Henry to do things, but it's different. With Don, I didn't even have to ask. He'd just come over. With Henry I have to specifically ask. Don was home all the time, so I could ask him and not feel so bad. Henry works these long hours, so I hesitate to ask him to do things for me.

Henry and I were standing by Don's bedside before we took him off the machines. Someone said, "If you want to say something to him, you'd better do it now." Henry said, "You've always been like a father to me." That made sense, because the twins were only four when our father died. Although I never thought of Don as a father, there was obviously some element of that because of my feelings of safety and security. Also, Don was the patriarch of the family. He did a lot of the planning, organizing, and communicating. Now that he's gone, who is going to do that, pick up the pieces? Don was fiercely committed to family. He didn't have a lot of friends. His family was everything. There was nothing he loved better. He loved his nieces and nephews. He was fierce about his own kids. He was a powerful force. There is constant talk about him when we get together. He was a creature of habit, rigid about many things, had weird little quirks, so there are endless stories to tell and laugh about, and maddening things, too. He was not this sweet, cuddly type. He could be that at times, but he had other not so pleasant sides. So there are lots of stories to tell. For a lot of reasons, I haven't been able to move into the position of family matriarch—doing things like having people over, taking my role as one of the aunts. I feel like I haven't been able to keep up my end of the bargain. Don's son is gradually moving into the role of family patriarch.

There's a constant theme in our family. Who's going to live; who's going to die; how's this all going to work? For me, it's trying to understand who I am and where I've come from. Losing my father when I did profoundly altered my sense of what I can count on. Being so young, I learned really bad things can happen. I can't just say everything will be okay, because it can be really bad. Unfortunately, I took that feeling much further than it needed to go. I'm always expecting the worst. If someone has the sniffles, I worry that it's pneumonia. If the phone rings after 9:00 at night, I worry it's a death. I know I've taken that type of thinking pretty far, but it's happened over and over again. I do treasure the little things, but I worry and always anticipate bad things. That doesn't serve me well. It's a constricted way of living. I often wish I could be freer or take risks. I don't mean like snowboarding, which I'd never do, but take a vacation that I wouldn't have taken or change jobs. Do something that scares me. I can never completely relax or feel free.

People talk about this as a growth experience; you'll come out of this a much stronger person. I hear this a lot. Your family will be closer. I'd be happy to be a weaker person if I could have my brothers back again. If I say things like, we were a close family but this made us closer, people will say, "Isn't that wonderful?" Well, no it isn't. I don't think people are trying to be insensitive. They're just trying to find something better that can come out of this.

21

DELILAH and MARTHA

Delilah, her three sisters and brother are a close-knit family, drawn together in the face of their parents' early deaths. The siblings enjoy each other's company and often plan family gatherings. Martha is the oldest of the siblings; Delilah is the second oldest.

Delilah is a good friend of mine. She is a high-energy person with a forcefully positive outlook on life. She has worked in the field of health education and so is quite knowledgeable about issues of health promotion and disease prevention. Her particular areas of interest and expertise are communication between health care providers and patients and medical ethics. She believes deeply in being an advocate for oneself and patient participation in making decisions about one's health care.

Delilah is the first person I interviewed when I decided to pursue this writing project. (When we discussed issues of anonymity, she gleefully told me to call her Delilah.) Our conversation took place in January 2002, two years after her older sister, Martha, was diagnosed with Stage 1 uterine cancer at the age of 55. Because the cancer was detected early and because the tumor was encapsulated, Martha's prognosis was very good. With internal and external post-surgical radiation, there was a 93% chance that the cancer would not recur.

At the time of Martha's diagnosis, Delilah and I had already had a number of conversations about Lilly's situation, as well as my own

reactions to Lilly's illness. I wanted to interview Delilah in a more
formal way, however, once she, too, was facing the potential loss
of a sibling. My sense was that a diagnosis like cancer catapults
family members into a new life space. Through the conversation
with Delilah I hoped to articulate more explicitly the thoughts and
feelings at play in this pre-dying space.

I first revisited the transcript of my interview with Delilah after
three years had passed. During that time, I accompanied Lilly
through what experts call the "trajectory of dying." During that
time, Delilah herself was diagnosed with breast cancer, underwent
a lumpectomy and radiation, and completed reconstructive surgery.
Now, as I turn again to the transcript, she is well past the five year
post-diagnosis and treatment milestone.

I began the conversation by saying, "I've been wondering if you
have the same sense that I do of time being bizarre. I'll begin to
look forward to some event, and then stop myself. By the time that
event happens, Lilly will be that much closer to dying. So the sense
of anticipation gets stopped. Have you experienced anything like
that?"

We're a real close family. We are always planning, like "Where's the next party. When are we going to get together?" Now, we're not saying those sorts of things, which is very strange. We'll say, "Won't it be great when we get together again?" Then we never move forward to make it happen.

Maybe we're thinking, "What if she's not good enough to be there. Then what kind of get-together would that be?" Or, maybe I'm noticing a real backing off, because of all the emotional and psychological stuff that's gone on with Martha's illness. I'm surprised at that. We're all just sort of biding our time to see what piece of bad news comes next.

Martha had surgery to correct adhesions caused by the radiation. That was successful, but she has not gotten better. About 10 days post-surgery she announced that, despite the fact that there was nothing physiologically wrong, she was no longer going to eat or drink. She says she has no appetite; eating makes her sick; the smell of it; the feel of it. She knows she should, but she just can't, and she's tired of people asking her about it. That was really astounding to us in more ways than one. We've always perceived Martha as resilient and fun and tough. She's not been that way since she's been sick. Then there's this other piece of her. She's had a history of depression, and a history of not quite an eating disorder, but an obsession with eating well. This was really irregular, very scary.

She went back to the hospital for three weeks. They fed her, gave her IVs, and finally said, "There's nothing physiologically wrong with you. You must go home." She said, "But I can't eat." They said, "Well, try." So that's where she is now. She's trying, but she's not real successful. We're all reading books trying to figure out what might be the matter. I'm thinking that she might have to get desperately ill again before anyone puts all of these pieces together.

Her doctors have said, "You're cured. There's no more cancer." When she began having these eating difficulties, she had surgery to remove adhesions caused by the radiation. The doctors said, "Gee, we're surprised that you can't eat or drink. When we opened you up, there were some adhesions, but we would have thought from your symptoms that it would have been much worse than it was." They have actually had an inside look, and they've done every other gastrointestinal test they can do. There is nothing physiologically wrong."

She's lost scads and scads of weight. She's gray. She looks like someone who is terminally ill with cancer. We're wondering, "Does she think she's terminal or has some lingering cancer not been found?"

Martha worked in a hospice where she had a friend who's into complementary and alternative medicine. She does a lot of hypnotism for people with cancer at the end of life to relieve their pain. Martha asked, "Did I think that was weird?" I said, "No, I thought that was okay. Whatever it takes." Then she said, "She's coming over to hypnotize my bowel." Martha's an intelligent person. She's been a really strange, but active partner in managing her illness. What struck me was that she called her friend from <u>hospice</u> who does this for <u>dying</u> people.

She has cast herself as helpless, as somewhat hopeless, as very needy. She would suck everybody in, but that's not who she is. She would have people take care of her, because she thinks she's going to die. I think she might if she continues to think this way. I have a sense of her slipping away.

Her most recent job with hospice was to develop a transitional care program for people who aren't officially ready to go into hospice. The hospice can contact you or you can contact the hospice. They will set you up with support services. Then when you're clearly in the dying process, it's more likely that you would go to that hospice, because those are the folks you've had some interaction with. It's interesting to me that now she seems to be tapping the services she was helping to create.

There's not a medical person in the world who's saying, "Martha, you're thriving." But they don't say—I don't know what they say. I'm not there to ask them. We've talked about contacting her surgeon or her internist. We haven't done it yet, and people have said, "Good luck with that." If her husband or children were to inquire, but siblings from the other side of the United States, they're probably not going to talk to us.

After her initial surgery she called all of us and said, "I don't think I'm going to do the radiation." We were stunned and said, "That's stupid. Why would you not do that?" Eventually she did have the external radiation, but never the internal. She said, "I've done my homework. I've checked this out. I'm not sure I need it." We said, "You must." She thought we would say, "That's okay." When we didn't, I think she felt a little betrayed.

The rest of Martha's life is not in good shape. Her marriage is in distress. I wonder if there is a substratum of depression. Lots of times she says, "I'm sort of like Mom." My mother had actually died of lung cancer. She also had some sort of eating related disorder, was very, very thin, weighed 89 pounds when she was older. There are some similarities, although my sister was a marathon runner, a healthy eater, always had great muscle mass, and was in great physical shape. She's taken to saying, "This is happening to me just like Mother."

I'm not quite sure what to say to her anymore. Is the loving response to say, "It's your choice; we're with you 100% of the way." Or is it sort of tough love, "Get a grip." We don't know. We're all really perplexed. We don't know what else to try to do. I have a feeling that if this happens a second time around, if another one of us gets sick, we'll do this better.

Before Martha had surgery to remove the cancer, she was working with hospice in California. One of the women she worked with was a member of a big, wonderful Baptist church. When this lady found out that Martha had cancer, she told some church ladies who make quilts for sick people. After a quilt is made, they hang it in the church sanctuary. They invited Martha to the church. She stood at the back, and the women carried a quilt like a huge banner and gave it to her. The quilt was all the colors, flowers and things that she likes on the front. On the backside was a large cross that signifies these ladies' faith. She was very touched, especially because she was not a member of the church, just a friend of a member.

Although I thought it was more appropriate for someone who was going to die, it was a beautiful gesture. It was also scary. We went to the wedding of Martha's daughter. In the midst of this wonderful party, she said, "You have to come and see my quilt." I said, "Did you bring it with you?" She said, "Yes. I can't leave home without it. It comes in the car if I'm going to the grocery store. I lay it over my body every night. I feel like a baby with a blankie." That's spooky to me. I am a very faith-filled person, but this was spooky.

To Martha it represents a very warm, loving, caring, supportive community. For my other sisters, my brother, and me, it took on a whole different dimension. When a Catholic person dies, they bring the casket into the church and lay a big white cloth over it. It is symbolic of the white garment they gave you when you were baptized, and then here you are at the end of your life. It's a great big white blanket, and it has a big cross on the top of it. The memory of that ritual is very keen to me from my parents' death. The symbolism was great. For my sister to take the quilt and lay it over herself is very significant for me. My other sister was at the wedding, too, and she felt exactly the same way, like "Oh, my God."

I doubt that Martha thinks, "This reminds me of the cloth they put over the casket." But I haven't talked to her about it. She loves it, feels protected and strengthened by it. It's just a great vignette to show where we are with her. We don't know whether to say, "Hey that's really great, but that spooked me." We're afraid if we said that it might hurt her feelings or take something valuable away from her. That ease of conversation is gone.

We have been a family that talks—A LOT. It's really strange that we are not talking, but then she's different. Her mental health is so strange. She's off in a lot of different directions so we never know if we're hitting the mark or not. Our ability to talk is disrupted. Now I'm wondering, "Were we not as grounded as I thought we were? Or has this been such a cataclysmic event that it's disrupted everything?" I'm not sure what the answer is.

My sisters, brother, and I probably talk at least five days a week. It's terrific that we're talking with each other, but we're all sort of a wreck. One person calls one person, then that person calls another one who calls someone else. "What did you hear; what did she say; what did she do? This is what I heard; that isn't what I heard." It's like two different stories to two different people. To one sister, she will say very little, because she thinks that sister won't hear it very well. My youngest sister is gentle and supportive, so she'll hear a lot of, "This is hard. I'm discouraged today. I'm not doing too well, but now you're here, and I'm going to feel better." The message to my brother is, "You know I'm still having a great time." The message to me is, "Just in case you think I sound better, I'm really not." Now bear in mind, this is a lot of talking. When there are five people and we're all speaking to her every two or three days, and then speaking to each other in between, then it's like that game where you whisper in each other's ears. Many times we'll say to each other, "WHAT? WHAT? That's not at all what I heard yesterday afternoon or this morning."

Maybe the idea that everybody would get the same message is not realistic. Sometimes we think it's because she's not 100% emotionally balanced. Other times I think, "Okay, she would share that kind of stuff with my brother. She would share this kind of stuff with me." But it isn't reassuring, because we don't know what the real story is.

We're really running without a script right now. There's no telling what it's going to be. It's very uncertain; it's very hard. We're still speaking to her, but I bet there are triple the number of conversations among ourselves as there are interactions with her. So we're talking about what she said to each other as much as we're talking with her.

This feels like how we were talking when my parents were dying. Like, "Oh my God, what's happening here; what are we going to do." We didn't make the outcome any different, but we had to keep going over it and over it and over it. That's what we're doing now with Martha.

Personally, this is much more scary than with my parents. Maybe that's why the conversation is so hot and heavy. We have a standing joke in our family that the lifeline isn't very long, genetically speaking. We have always said, "Let's have a rip roaring 50s, because the 60s aren't a pretty picture." We've laughed about that over the years. Now the oldest of us sick and it's like, "holy shmoly; what is this?" It is very hard to have a sibling who is desperately ill, because it just makes you realize that you may not have much time. Then again, you could have another ten or twenty years, who's to say? Despite the fact she's the eldest, we wouldn't have expected her to have health problems. We would have expected several others to have them, but not her.

Last week we sort of came to a pact. We were all getting pretty obsessed with this. These daily conversations with 3 or 4 people, all saying, "How do you think she's sounded today?" So we said we're just going to wait it out. That decision was huge, waiting to hear the next bad thing. Because obviously we cannot stop whatever that is, because it sort of has a life of its own.

POSTSCRIPT: Several years after this interview, Martha was diagnosed with early on-set Alzheimer's. Delilah and I have speculated that Martha's troubling behaviors may have been early indications of the disease. In retrospect Delilah also believes her sister was profoundly depressed. As she told me, "Martha's was a balancing act on shifting sands—her physical illness, her troubled marriage, her scattered thought processes, her faltering sense of self. Martha finally found peace in embracing a new role as an Alzheimer's crusader. Between 2006 and 2010, she was active as a member of the Alzheimer's Association Early Onset Advisory Group; her story became part of Story Corps' online resources; she was interviewed as a part of a PBS special on memory loss in America, and she and her husband were featured in Time magazine. She loved the attention, and she did a great job. To me, this is very interesting. I have often reminded people in a support group setting that THEY ARE NOT THEIR DISEASE. In the case of my sister, she finally rested when she became the voice of hers. The lessons in the waiting room of death are still unfolding for me and my siblings, and we are still working to understand them."

Epilogue

As I draw this writing project to a close, the 14th anniversary of my sister's death has passed. Over the years, my grief has oxidized, muting the pain of the initial loss. Still, I don't experience this as "getting beyond" or "getting through" grief. I resonate with the outrage expressed by several surviving siblings who resented the medicalization of grief, as though it is a pathology that must be cured. A shift occurred in the deepest foundations of our being. Even if just for a moment, the stark reality of our own vulnerability, our own mortality, shattered illusions of invincibility. The constellation of family relationships was irrevocably disrupted; family traditions will never again hold the same meaning. Regardless of one's religious beliefs or the specific circumstances of a sibling's death, the "why questions"—why her/him and not me, why now, why so sudden or lingering—precipitate a search to make meaning of the loss. These existential disruptions offer an opportunity to look more deeply into ourselves and how we want to live our lives. Do we face our anxieties or let them overwhelm us? Do we hold grudges or reach out and weave caring relationships? Do we express our love or remain haunted by the question, "Did they know how much they meant to us?" How can I live without regrets? What legacies did my sibling leave and what will be my legacy? In what ways can I honor my sibling's life? I was deeply touched by the ways in which my interviewees expressed such thoughts and feelings. All were hesitant to give advice, recognizing that each person's experience of loss and grief is different. Taken together, our experiences do not constitute a set of guidelines by which to "get through grief." Rather, our stories offer reassurance that we are not alone in the pain of our loss. As essayist Barry Lopez[13] says,

> The stories people tell have a way of taking care of them. If stories come to you, care for them. And learn to give them away where they are needed. Sometimes a person needs a story more than food to stay alive. That is why we put these stories in each other's memory. This is how people care for themselves.

I carry with me these stories of siblings whose deaths came too early and too hard. The memories shared by their surviving brothers and sisters have mingled with my own memories, becoming part of me, just as surely as Lilly is still with me, shaping and reshaping my understanding of life, myself, and my place in the world.

---

13 Barry Lopez, *Crow & Weasel,* New York: North Point Press, 1990.

Bibliography

This bibliography is not an exhaustive list of references on death, dying, grief, and loss. Although I have grouped the references according to broad themes, the categories are neither definitive nor mutually exclusive. They are meant to help readers locate materials that might be most helpful.

SIBLING LOSS

Ascher, Barbara Lazear. *Landscape without Gravity: A Memoir of Grief.* New York: Penguin Books, 1993.

Becvar, Dorothy S. "When a Sibling Dies," *In the Presence of Grief: Helping Family Members Resolve Death, Dying and Bereavement Issues.* New York: Guildford Press, 2003.

Cole, Natalie. *Love Brought Me Back: A Journey of Loss and Gain.* New York: Simon & Schuster, 2010.

Davies, Bette. *Shadows in the Sun: The Experiences of Sibling Bereavement in Childhood* (Series in Death, Dying and Bereavement). Philadelphia: Brunner-Routledge Books, 1998.

DeVita-Raeburn, Elizabeth. *The Empty Room: Surviving the Loss of a Brother or Sister at Any Age.* New York: Scribner, 2004.

Donnelly, Katherine Fair. *Recovering from the Loss of a Sibling.* San Jose, CA: toExcel, 2000.

Fanos, Joanna H. *Sibling loss.* Mahwah, NJ: Lawrence Erlbaum Associates, 1996.

Farrant, Ann. *Sibling Bereavement: Helping Children Cope with Loss.* (2nd Ed.). Hertfordshire, England, 1998.

Fell, Lynda Cheldelin. *Grief Diaries: Loss of a Sibling*. Ferndale, WA: AlyBlue Media, 2015.

John's Sister. *The Forgotten Mourners: Sibling Survivors of Suicide*. Denver: Outskirts Pres, 2012.

Miller, Sara Swan. *An Empty Chair: Living in the Wake of a Sibling's Suicide*. San Jose, CA: Writers Club Press, 2000.

Neufield, Elsie K. & Augsburger, David. *Dancing in the Dark: A Sister Grieves*. PA: Herald Press, 1990.

Rosen, Helen. *Unspoken Grief: Coping with Childhood Sibling Loss*. 1990.

Ruiz, Ruth Ann. *Coping with the Death of a Brother or Sister*. New York: The Rosen Publishing Group, 2001.

White, P. Gill. *Sibling Grief: Healing after the Death of a Sister or Brother*. Lincoln, NE: iUniverse, 2006.

Wolfelt, Alan D. *Healing the Adult Sibling's Grieving Heart: 100 Practical Ideas after Your Brother or Sister Dies*. Ft. Collins, CO: Companion Press, 2008.

Wray, T.J. *Surviving the Death of a Sibling: Living through Grief when an Adult Brother or Sister Dies*. NY: Three Rivers Press, 2003.

GENERAL BOOKS ON LOSS & DEATH

Atwater, P.M.H. with David H. Morgan. *The Complete Idiot's Guide to Near-Death Experiences*. Indianapolis, IN: Alpha Books, 2000.

Baugher, Bob. *A Guide for the Bereaved Survivor: A List of Reactions, Suggestions and Steps for Coping with Grief*. New Castle: WA, 1998, 2013.

Becker, Ernest. *The Denial of Death*. New York: Macmillan. 1973.

Jose, Stephanie. *Progressing through Grief: Guided Exercises to Understand Your Emotions and Recover from Loss*. Berkeley, CA: Althea Press, 2016.

Noel, Brook & Blair, Pamela D. *I Wasn't Ready to Say Goodbye: Surviving, Coping and Healing after the Sudden Death of a Loved One*. Napersville, IL: Sourcebooks, Inc., 2000.

DeSpelder, Lynne Ann, & Strickland, Albert Lee. *The Last Dance: Encountering Death and Dying*. Sixth Edition. Boston: McGraw Hill, 2000.

Didion, Joan. *The Year of Magical Thinking*. New York: Alfred A. Knopf, 2005.

Dunne, Edward J., John L. McIntosh, & Karen Dunne-Maxim (Eds.). *Suicide and its Aftermath: Understanding and Counseling the Survivors*. New York: W.W. Norton & Co., 1987.

Groopman, Jerome. *The Measure of Our Days: New Beginnings at Life's End.* New York: Viking, 1997.

Kavanaugh, Robert E. *Facing Death.* Baltimore, MD: Penguin Books, 1972.

Kubler-Ross, Elisabeth. *On Death and Dying: What the Dying Have to Teach Doctors, Nurses, Clergy, and Their Own Families.* New York: Simon & Schuster, 1969.

Kubler-Ross, Elisabeth. *The Wheel of Life: A Memoir of Living and Dying.* New York: Touchstone, 1997.

Levang, Elizabeth & Ilse, Sherokee. *Remembering with Love: Messages of Hope for the First Year of Grieving and Beyond.* Minneapolis, MN: Fairview Press, 1992.

Lord, Janice Harris. *No Time for Goodbyes: Coping with Sorrow, Anger, and Injustice after a Tragic Death.* (5th Edition). 2014.

Mehran, Elizabeth. *After the Darkest Hour the Sun Will Shine Again: A Parent's Guide to Coping with the Loss of a Child.* New York: Simon & Schuster, 1997.

Palmer, Laura. *Shrapnel in the Heart: Letters and Remembrances from the Vietnam Veterans Memorial.* New York: Vintage Books, 1987.

Romanyshyn, Robert. *The Soul in Grief: Love, Death and Transformation.* Berkeley, CA: Frog Ltd., 1999.

Turkle, Studs. *Will the Circle be Unbroken? Reflections on Death, Rebirth, and Hunger for a Faith.* New York: The New Press, 2001.

Walton, Charlie. *When There are No Words: Finding Your Way to Cope with Loss and Grief.* Ventura, CA: Pathfinder Publishing of California, 1996.

Welshons, John E. *Awakening from Grief: Finding the Road back to Joy.* Makawao, Maui, HI: Inner Ocean Publishing, 2003.

PERSONAL EXPERIENCES OF CHRONIC & TERMINAL ILLNESS

Carel, Havi. *Illness: The Cry of the Flesh: The Art of Living.* Stocksfield: Acumen, 2008.

Dresser, R. (Ed.). *Malignant: Medical Ethicists Confront Cancer.* New York: Oxford University Press, 2012.

Frank, Arthur W. *At the Will of the Body: Reflections on Illness.* Boston: Houghton Mifflin, 1991.

Frank, Arthur W. *The Wounded Storyteller: Body, Illness, and Ethics.* Chicago: The University of Chicago Press, 1995.

Ofri, Danielle. *What Doctors Feel: How Emotions Affect the Practice of Medicine.* Boston: Beacon Press, 2013.

Hitchens, Christopher. *Mortality.* New York: Twelve, 2012.

Palmer, Laura. *Shrapnel in the Heart: Letters and Remembrances from the Vietnam Veterans Memorial.* New York: Vintage, 1987.

Rothenberg, Laura. *Breathing for a Living: A Memoir.* New York: Hyperion, 2003.

Shavelson, Lonny. *A Chosen Death: The Dying Confront Assisted Suicide.* New York: Simon & Schuster, 1995.

Weinholtz, Donn. *Longing to Live...Learning to Die.* San Jose, CA: Writers Club Press, 2002.

Willis, Peter & Leeson, Kate (Eds.). *Learning Life from Illness Stories.* Mt. Gravatt, Queenland, Australia: Post Press, 2012

SEARCH FOR MEANING & FAITH

Albom, Mitch. *The Five People You Meet in Heaven.* New York: Hyperion, 2003.

Beck, Martha. *Finding Your Own North Star: Claiming the Life You Were Meant to Live.* New York: Crown Publishers, 2001.

Brehony, Kathleen A. *After the Darkest Hour: How Suffering Begins the Journey to Wisdom.* New York: Henry Holt and Company, 2000.

Brehony, Kathleen A. *Awakening at Midlife: A Guide to Reviving Your Spirit, Recreating Your Life, and Returning to Your Truest Self.* New York: Riverhead Books, 1996.

Cathcart, Thomas & Klein, Daniel. *Heidegger and a Hippo Walk through Those Pearly Gates: Understanding Philosophy (and Jokes!) to Explore Life, Death, the Afterlife, and Everything in Between.* New York: Penguin Books, 2009.

Chopra, Deepak. *Life after Death: The Burden of Proof.* New York: Harmony Books, 2006.

Crandell, Susan. *Thinking about Tomorrow: Reinventing Yourself at Midlife.* New York: Warner Wellness, 2007.

Davidson, Sara. *Leap! What Will We Do with the Rest of Our Lives? Reflections from the Boomer Generation.* New York: Random House, 2007.

Dorff, Elliot N. *The Jewish Approach to Repairing the World (Tikkun Olam).* Woodstock, VT: Jewish Lights Publishing, 2008.

Edward, John. *After Life: Answers from the Other Side.* New York: Princess Books, 2003

Fowler, James W. *Stages of Faith: The Psychology of Human Development and the Quest for Meaning.*

San Francisco: HarperCollins, 1995.

Frankl, Viktor E. *Man's Search for Meaning*. New York: Pocket Books, 1939.

Gerzon, Robert. *Finding Serenity in the Age of Anxiety*. New York: Macmillan, 1997.

Klein, Daniel. *Travels with Epicurus: A Journey to a Greek Island in Search of a Fulfilled Life*. New York: Penguin Books, 2012.

Klein, Daniel. *Every Time I find the Meaning of Life, They Change It. Wisdom of the Great Philosophers on How to Live*. New York: Penguin Books, 2015.

Kushner, Harold S. *Living a Life that Matters: Resolving the Conflict between Conscience and Success*. New York: Alfred A. Knopf. 2001.

LaMott. Anne. *Traveling Mercies: Some Thoughts on Faith*. New York: Anchor Books, 1999.

Schwartz, Gary. E. with William L. Simon. *The Afterlife Experiments: Breakthrough Scientific Evidence of Life after Death*. New York: Pocket Books, 2002.

Singh, Kathleen Dowling. *The Grace in Dying: A Message of Hope, Comfort, and Spiritual Transformation*. San Francisco, CA: HarperCollins, 1998.

Watts, Alan W. *The Wisdom of Insecurity: A Message for an Age of Anxiety*. New York: Vintage Books, 1951.

Wiesel, Elie. *Night/Dawn/Day*. Northvale, NJ: Jason Aronson, Inc., 1985.

Acknowledgements

I am indebted to many individuals for their help, support, and encouragement. The courage, grace and wisdom of those who shared their stories of sibling loss sustained me during dark hours of grief and despair. My sense of obligation for their generosity pushed me to resume this writing project when it would have been easier to avoid the sadness and pain of revisiting my loss and theirs. Although I used pseudonyms throughout Part 2 of the book, I had asked each person I interviewed if they would prefer to remain anonymous or be identified by name. The following chose to be recognized:

Interviewee:	Liz Allen Campbell
Sibling:	Michelle
Interviewee:	Jean Fortina
Sibling:	Victoria Downey
Interviewee:	Jean H. Henderson
Sibling:	Nancy Humason Lee
Interviewee:	Roger P. Howard
Siblings:	Harold Howard
	Ruth Howard Trent
Interviewee:	Marjorie Logsdon
Sibling:	Helen
Interviewee:	Susan D. Scherpereel
Sibing:	Mary Ann Becklenberg
Interviewee:	Mary Sciulli
Sibling:	Tom Sciulli

Interviewee:	Tracy Smith
Sibling:	Michelle Brosh
Interviewee:	Sue Zola
Sibling:	Bill

Four additional interviewees preferred to remain anonymous. Several individuals had agreed to be interviewed, but before I could arrange a time to talk with them, my sister's condition worsened and I went to be with her. After Lilly died, I had neither the intellectual or emotional energy to accept their offers. I hope they have forgiven my lack of follow through.

I am grateful to the many friends who listened patiently and kindly to my angst-filled conversations as I coped with feelings of despair. In particular, Sue Scherpereel and JoAnn Giglio offered not only countless hours of support, but also wise counsel.

During the final preparation of the book, many friends generously gave their time and attention to provide feedback and proofread drafts. I appreciate the assistance of Wendy Bell, Pat Buddemeyer, Karen Bilcsik, Dorothy Gold, Jane Hadburg, Bob Metz, Pam Morrison, Lynn Richards, Kathy Rizzo, Micheline Stabile, and Elise Yoder. I appreciate the help and guidance provided by Mike Murray of Pearhouse Productions in the technical production of the book.

Some debts run so deep, they can never be repaid. My gratitude towards Lilly's husband, Tom Walker, is one such debt. His steadfast care during Lilly's struggle to survive and then her months of dying was such an act of selfless love and devotion. I am pleased, and know Lilly would be pleased, that Tom has remarried and found happiness with Linda, a wonderful woman who also knows the pain of losing a spouse. She honors Lilly's memory and has warmly embraced me as a member of her family.

Finally, I am deeply grateful to my husband, Earl Novendstern, who respected my need to be with Lilly during her final months. He coped graciously and lovingly during the months we were separated and offered comfort and support when I returned home.

Learning Moments Press

Learning Moments Press is an independent publishing company dedicated to sharing the wisdom that comes from thoughtful reflection on experience. The Wisdom of Life Series offers insightful reflections on significant life events that challenge the meaning of one's life, one's sense of self, and one's place in the world.

Cooligraphy artist Daniel Nie created the logo for Learning Moments Press by combining two symbol systems. Following the principles of ancient Asian symbolism, Daniel framed the logo with the initials of Learning Moments Press. Within this frame, he has replicated the Adinkra symbol for *Sankofa* as interpreted by graphic artists at the Documents and Designs Company. As explained by Wikipedia, Adinkra is a writing system of the Akan culture of west Africa. *Sankofa* symbolizes taking from the past what is good and bringing it into the present in order to make positive progress through the benevolent use of knowledge. Inherent in this philosophy is the belief that the past illuminates the present and that the search for knowledge is a life-long process.